In this evolving industry, it's both refreshing and reassuring to find people like Bruce leading the charge on researching fields outside of our own to better shape how we influence security culture and behaviour.

Keeping a wider perspective and the end goal of positive security culture change in mind only serves to benefit us, and **this book is the perfect combination of easily digestible reflection, information and valuable recommendations** and actions for senior leaders, CISOs, CIOs and security awareness professionals alike.

Louise Cockburn
Education & Awareness Manager, Burberry

An **insightful and highly informative** read for security practitioners, business leaders, psychologists and behavioural scientists alike.

Re-Thinking The Human Factor explores more than just cyber security, it delves into the behavioural and cultural aspects of building, influencing and managing meaningful messages.

Highly recommended A*!

Inderpal Dhami, IBM Security

In this book, Bruce makes security personal and highlights the human factor element that runs through everything we do as security professionals, whether we acknowledge it or not.

The book demonstrates how important is to listen rather than just broadcast, and to think about not just WHAT we want to say but HOW we should say it. And why we need to resist the temptation to just fall back on technology measures or let user awareness become a compliance box-ticking exercise.

Bruce shows us how, as security professionals, we can up our game and get better results for the organisations that hire us. He explores many areas of interpersonal communication to create a clear understanding of why these play such a vital part in grabbing the attention of the audience. **He succinctly explains how we can make the rules easy to understand** - and act on - and establishing the part everyone must play to make it work.

I thoroughly enjoyed reading this book and, although I like to think of myself as having a pragmatic and empathetic approach to infosec, there is always more to learn and **I have certainly come away with some more ideas of how communicate more effectively, change behaviours and nurture a good culture of security.**

Matt Gordon-Smith
CISO, Anglo American

RE-THINKING THE HUMAN FACTOR

A Philosophical Approach to Information Security
Awareness Behaviour and Culture

BRUCE HALLAS

Published by The Hallas Institute, UK.

For permission requests or bulk orders contact the publisher by writing to hello@hallasinstitute.com

Visit the author's websites at www.brucehallas.com and www.marmaladebox.com

First edition.

ISBN 978-1-9996955-0-7

Disclaimer:

Every effort has been made to ensure that the information contained within this book is accurate at the time of going to production, and the publisher or author cannot accept responsibility for any errors or omissions, however caused. No responsibility for loss or damage occasioned to any person acting or refraining from action as a result of the material in this book can be accept by the editor, publisher or the author.

Credits:

Book cover design by Martin Knox and editing by Ian Phillipson

RE-THINKING THE HUMAN FACTOR

The world as we have created it is a process of our thinking. It cannot be changed without changing our thinking.

Albert Einstein

Contents

Chapter One

If humans can make it,
humans can break it.

The Case For Change

In a democracy, committees are often the tool of choice for legislatures looking to hold the great and the good to account. In the United States, Congressional Committees can subpoena witnesses to appear before them. In the UK, attendance is more by 'informal request', an invitation only a few refuse.

These committees do their work in places such as the monolithic Dirksen Senate Office Building in Washington DC's Capitol Complex, or the House of Commons historic Committee Rooms. It's here that corporate leaders can find themselves under the microscope, answering questions on topics of national importance.

Given the threat of increasingly sophisticated and significant cyber attacks on critical infrastructure[1], data security is now one of these, an ever-hotter hot potato governments are taking more and more seriously.

That means CEOs and other executives can no longer hide in the shadows from this new and ever evolving security reality. Unless you can show you have done all you reasonably can to mitigate a potential risk, and justify their decisions, then they will have a problem.

What's more, committees are no respecters of reputation. So, even as I'm writing this book, data privacy is in the headlines with Mark Zuckerburg, CEO of Facebook facing questions from members of the Senate committee. His 'rabbit caught in the headlights expression' showed that even for those prepared for the challenge, appearing before a committee can be exceptionally uncomfortable experience.

Whatever the topic, whoever they are 'grilling', the committee format tends to be the same. A panel of MPs or Senators sits facing the witness.

After a preamble and introductions, a Q&A session follows during which witnesses are expected to answer "carefully, fully and honestly" questions like these ...

Senator/MP:

As CEO, did you consider this a potential information security threat?

A reasonable question. Part of the job of a CEO is to manage organisational risk which means that ultimate responsibility for cyber security must lie with you[2]. Dido Harding, one-time CEO of telecoms provider TalkTalk, acknowledged that fact to a committee of British MPs. So, CEOs can't claim with any confidence that data breaches fall into someone else's domain, like the CISO.

Senator/MP:

Did you make sufficient effort to identify vulnerabilities in your information security systems and processes?

Obviously not. For too many companies, protecting data has long been considered something of a tick box exercise. It can't be anymore. Now you must be able to reassure any MP or Senator, with the bit between their teeth, that you have done your very best to create a robust security environment. If you can't, then don't expect to get an easy ride.

Senator/MP:
Did you properly evaluate the likelihood of this threat happening and the impact if it did?

This nasty question should send shivers down the spine of most CEOs because it cuts to the core of what you consider an acceptable risk when it comes to protecting data.

Sadly, the truth is that usually you could have done more but chose not to because of cost, pragmatism or your attitude to risk. You may have thought an event would never happen or that you could ride it out if it did. But that's only a viable position until something happens.

In response to such a question, you brazen it out by taking the "there was no more we could have done" approach. This position is only really tenable if you know without a doubt that you have done all you can … or you feel in a particularly combative mood.

Or instead, you could choose the path more trodden by saying: "I'm sorry. We made mistakes and we will learn the lessons from this accordingly."

This 'mea culpa' approach as was the one that Zucker-berg when he was forced into his embarrassing 'data apology tour'.

This involved saying sorry (a lot) for presiding over a platform that was described as "a twisted tool for propaganda, harassment and the mass theft of personal information"[3]. So much for the company's ambition of bringing the world together.

Senator/MP:

Did you communicate the potential of this threat to your board and risk owners?

If you are CEO or CISO and you didn't, then you probably should have. Unfortunately, most CISOs still have too little 'face time' with the board. That means many companies only wake up to the need for good CISO-CEO communication after an event.

 And of course, there may be an implicit (sometimes explicit) signal from the board that they don't actually want to hear what they consider yet another security scare story.

Senator/MP:

How did you decide if this was or wasn't an acceptable risk?

Another tricky question that exposes your organisation's risk profile by revealing what you think important and what you don't. This question forces you to disclose the process by which you identified your appetite for risk. In other words, how willing you are to play fast and loose with information. Having this on public display could be rather embarrassing.

Senator/MP:
Did you identify and implement appropriate control policies, processes and procedures, and were these controls implemented and maintained effectively, and periodically reviewed?

While legislators don't expect total security, they do expect every reasonable attempt to be made to keep data safe. Of course, if you don't have the controls in place, then you aren't managing your risk in line with your appetite.

Senator/MP:
Did you consider the possibility people wouldn't comply with your policies, procedures, processes and standards?

This is another tough one. Say 'yes' and someone is sure to ask what you then did to reduce the likelihood of non-compliance. Say 'no' and it can make you look as though you're behind the curve. The 'defence' of most CEOs, of course, will be that they are delivering an ongoing programme of security awareness. But just doing more of the same isn't a solution. When employees didn't comply with what was expected of them the first time around, they are hardly likely to do so the second. That makes throwing more and more education and awareness around a less than satisfactory response. This is akin to saying that just 'trying is good enough'… but it's not.

Senator/MP:

Have you made any comprehensive attempt to identify and address the root causes as to why people may not comply with your information security policies?

Again, in many instances, the truthful answer will be 'no'. But that's no longer a satisfactory or acceptable response given the decades of behavioural research that now enable us to increasingly understand what influences people to act in the way they do.

And since we are increasingly able to appreciate the root causes of why many employees 'reject' infosec, we are much better equipped to develop effective programmes of change. All this makes the human factor very much central to bringing about real and sustainable improvements in information security and not something inconsequential that sits at the periphery.

Given this, it's simply no defence to say that what's often called 'the human factor' is an uncontrollable variable that can't be managed and therefore make little or no attempt to do so.

Of course, as no system's totally effective there will always be residual risk whatever's done. Even after education and awareness programmes have been rolled out to help ensure personnel know their roles and responsibilities there will be non-compliance among some.

But if organisations acknowledge they can manage the human factor and look for ways to do so, not only will they achieve much better results but also, should there be an incident, be able to truthfully say that 'yes we have made users aware of their roles and responsibilities.' and we've given them the best opportunity to make a positive security choice. That's a genuine shift in accountability from employer to employee, and a transition from 'old' to 'new' ways of thinking about infosec.

The ever-greater scrutiny organisations are coming under means that managing information risk is much more important than it was even just five years ago. It certainly wasn't so high on the corporate agenda when I joined what was then called the IT security industry some 20 years ago.

I'd been hired by a value-added reseller to evaluate the market for IT security and storage, though most of my focus was on selling kit rather than research or consultancy. I certainly wasn't traditional information technology material with my degree in law, finance and marketing. But, given my background, I was naturally drawn to the legal and regulatory complexities around confidentiality, availability and integrity of data.

I also saw that when it came to information security, there was a world of difference between where organisations were and where they wanted to be. That led me to think, more and more, that we needed to see cyber security as a business performance issue, rather than an IT problem.

I also noticed that there was also a considerable disconnect between awareness and behaviour. So, I began asking myself *why* people *do* what they do, rather than what they are *supposed* to do.

From an industry perspective, this was all about human error and misjudgement with a widespread acceptance that these were unfixable flaws. People were considered a problem that couldn't be corrected other than through the use of a 'blunt instrument'.

Some time ago, I remember seeing a cartoon in an industry magazine that depicted a boxing ring. In corner A' was an IT 'heavyweight', in the other a hapless end user who was about to be taught an infosec lesson. If there was ever a metaphor for the way our industry perceived itself and what it was all about, then this was it.

But by assuming 'force' was the only way to bring about behavioural change, were we continuing to bark up the wrong tree? Were we just seeing 'users' as *the* problem but then failing to equip them with the capacity to become part of the solution? How could people make more positive choices about security behaviour when we never gave them the opportunity to do so.

Did we instead need to change our priorities? To move away from using ineffective one-off and irregular training in an effective attempt to make employees follow security policies? Were we missing a trick by focusing too much on technology as the solution, and putting insufficient emphasis on people?

Questions like these led me about six years ago to begin investing time into researching, thinking and developing my ideas about this 'human factor'. As my research progressed, I became increasingly aware of infosec's traditional flaws and better able to understand the reasons behind these weaknesses. And as I did so, I also began to see potential solutions.

Eventually, I developed a new model of information security – SABC™ (Security Awareness Behaviour Culture) – that doesn't just make people aware of best practice but also influences their behaviour for the better. This book embodies much of this new 'philosophy'.

It's one I hope will encourage a change in thinking

that places much more emphasis on what I consider to be the missing component in information security awareness ... the human factor.

It is obvious that as an industry we face a significant challenge. CISOs look to counter them using the many tools and strategies at their disposal, such as intrusion detection and prevention systems, defence in depth, active defence, red teams, penetration testing, bug bounties and the like. These still have their place. But the continuing 'defeats' that we suffer show that these are not a complete solution to our problems. Far from it. (Chapter 1)

Therefore, we cannot keep doing what we have always done by continuing to see information security simply as a technology problem, or just paying lip service to people and processes. I would say that our technology-first approach is a 'broken solution' that often results in over-complication. What we actually need in our increasingly complex world are simpler solutions. (Chapter 2)

So, rather than continue attempting to create a specific security culture, instead we need to focus on establishing a new organisational culture in which information security is naturally embedded. We tend to think of security as something separate, we shouldn't because it isn't. (Chapter 3)

Infosec's natural tendency is to turn to technology, so naturally we recruit primarily those with technological skills. That leads to a lack of diversity within our teams. This constrains our thinking and limits our capacity to handle the 'human factor', which I see as a fundamental component when it comes to risk mitigation. (Chapter 4)

If we are to become more effective, then we need to hire those who can better understand why we have collectively failed to bring about change in information security awareness, behaviour and culture, or to provide more effective solutions. (Chapter 5)

So, we need those from non-technical disciplines, who can re-design our systems and processes by calling on a new set of tools that draw on the latest insights from neuroscience, behavioural science and economics, psychology and semiotics to help 'make the right behaviour the easiest behaviour'. (Chapter 6) This is even more crucial in a fast-changing work environment that is being disrupted by independent contractors, personnel with multiple jobs, remote working and more.

There is always the question of how to get sceptical employees to buy into this new brand of information security. If we want to reinforce and influence behaviours that protect your organisation, then we need to speak in a way that our audience understands. All too often we don't. And if others don't appreciate the importance of information security, it will have little value to them. This requires a different communication approach, borrowing from other sectors who understand how small details can have a tremendous influence on behaviours. (Chapter 7)

For many organisations, particularly those without the luxury of a dedicated CISO, taking control of the human factor will not be an easy solution, but that is no reason not to try. It's certainly a challenge that can't be ignored.

Redesigning policy and process to bring greater awareness and behavioural change will require a different mindset and a fresh set of skills, both of which our own SABC™ programmes are specifically designed to develop. My work with organisations in the UK,

Europe, Asia and the US shows me that there is a rapidly growing appetite for this new approach. And not just from organisations, but also savvy security professionals who see the tide turning and wish to position themselves to better meet the new challenges that will inevitably face our industry.

In this book, I've set out my thoughts on the need for a more holistic approach, one that doesn't consider information security as some bolt-on feature but regards it instead an integral component of business.

'Rethinking the Human Factor' is for anyone involved in the information security awareness industry. That includes CIOs, CTOs and CISOs who own the strategy, as well as the increasing number of managers and independent consultants responsible for education, awareness and behaviour change programmes.

I hope it will be of particular interest if you are a key individual within an organisation who appreciates the need for a new way of thinking and a willingness to become the champion of the human factor.

So, perhaps we should begin this journey by looking at why we need a new information awareness security framework in the first place.

Chapter Two

"If the rate of change on the outside exceeds the rate of change on the inside, the end is near."

Jack Welch, former Chairman & CEO of General Electric

A Scan of the Information Security Landscape

I n 2017, data breaches were happening at twice the rate[4] of the year before. And almost half (46%) of all businesses had experienced at least one cyber-security breach in the previous 12 months[5].

Each of these is a failure with consequences, not least in lost sales — 86% of consumers say we won't do business with a company that suffers a data breach[6], especially if this involves loss of credit card details. Then there are the associated expenses: installing extra security, publicity and legal costs, as well as paying data protection fines. They all add up.

IBM in its 2017 Cost of Data Breach Study put the average cost globally of an information violation at $3.62 million. The Ponemon Institute puts it even higher[7] — $7.35 million — with each compromised identity costing an organisation $225. A new record! In heavily regulated sectors the figures are even higher — $336 in financial services and $380 in health care.

But often it's not to an organisation's bottom line that the greatest long-term damage is done, but to its reputation. Strategic research firm Forbes Insights says 46% of organisations suffered reputational damage because of an information breach[8], and that was back in 2014. What would that figure be now, given that data breaches make the headlines every week?

Among Facebook users in the US, 9% have deleted their accounts and 35% reduced their usage because of concerns over privacy concerns. These numbers are significant and a sign that privacy of data is now in the spotlight as never before. For all our misgivings about Facebook's approach, we can at least be grateful for their role in raising awareness of this issue.

Things are made worse when companies identify breaches late, then respond inadequately. That provokes the wrath of indignant journalists who throw coal on the fire. More negative media coverage then leads to customers voting with their feet. Data breaches are on a par with environmental disasters[9] when it comes to turning customers off.

"Three decades ago, up to 95% of the average corporation's value consisted of tangible assets. Today, 75% of the average corporation's value is intangible."

Thomson Reuters & Interbrand

As data breaches become more frequent and significant, the potential damage to society increases.

In 2015, hackers hit Ukraine's power grid, leaving more than 225,000 people without power. The following year, cyber criminals stole millions of dollars[10] through the global banking system SWIFT. Other state-sponsored attacks on the UK and US energy sectors have highlighted the susceptibility of critical infrastructures. Additionally, political 'information black ops' are compromising voting systems.

In October 2017, Head of Policy for the City of London Mark Boleat warned that cyber criminals would bring about the next financial crisis by "destroying bank records and changing the amounts people have in their accounts."

Benjamin Lawsky, superintendent of the New York State Department of Financial Services and one of America's most influential financial regulators, gave a similar warning. He said it was only a "matter of time" before there was an "Armageddon-style" cyber-attack on the global financial system.

The failure of security initiatives and programmes leads some to indulge in what's been dubbed 'security nihilism'. We assume that the world is full of genius hackers and that every threat will lead to the worst-case scenario.

Such fears feed a growing appetite among legislators, politicians and regulators to tighten their grip on those who fail to protect the data they hold. This is being reflected in a new legislative agenda that goes beyond a reliance on National Institute of Standards and Technology (NIST) guidelines and ISO27001. This international standard for information security management now includes a requirement for education and awareness to be demonstrably implemented and interestingly, this needs to be aligned ultimately to risk.

The General Data Protection Regulation (GDPR), which came into force on 25th May 2018 is designed to harmonise European data privacy laws and establish a much more rigorous approach to protecting the personal information of EU citizens, and it is going to affect organisations of all sizes. And, by requiring organisations to demonstrate effective security awareness, it highlights a growing acceptance of the role that security awareness plays in managing the risk of security and privacy breaches.

In Australia, the Notifiable Data Breaches (NDB) scheme requires those covered by the Privacy Act to notify those whose personal information is involved in a data breach when it's likely to result in "serious harm".

There are many who feel a tipping point's been reached, with increasingly vigorous calls for a 'digital protection agency' to "clean up toxic data spills, educate the public, and calibrate and levy fines"[11].

"Facebook is no longer a company; it's so powerful it should be considered its own country."[12]

Senator John Kennedy, Louisiana

It means business leaders must now allocate adequate time and resources to neutralising cyber security threats, or face the prospect of increased liability, hefty fines or worse.

Ultimately, how firms manage and react to risk depends largely on how likely it is they think things will go wrong ... and the downside if they do.

At a corporate level, this is normally enshrined in a standard control framework of policies, processes and procedures that determine and reflect what level of risk a business will tolerate and be comfortable with.

But often, rather than looking to prevent risk events happening in the first place, the emphasis seems to be more on managing them, so those involved aren't exposed to their after-effects. Such a cavalier approach potentially opens the door to vulnerabilities either maliciously exploited or accidentally exposed.

As a result, an organisation's leadership often sees and treats even significant breaches as 'collateral damage'. A short-term inconvenience, before it's back to business as usual.

And to an extent, this is often true. Stock prices do recover. Stakeholders are appeased. Old customers will forgive. New clients still come along.

eBay is still around after details of 145 million users were compromised in May 2014. The then CEO, John Donahue, described the breach as having 'little impact on the bottom line', with revenues in line with expectations.

And Sony's share price is now some two and half times higher than it was in April 2011, when 77 million PlayStation Network accounts were hacked. That led to the site being down for a month and estimated losses of $171 million.

'Bad stuff does happen. However, just accepting this with a shrug of the shoulders isn't effective risk management. What's needed instead is to better understand the root causes of residual risk and the options for dealing with it.

Given the constantly evolving world we live in, we must become better at information security awareness. In other words, the knowledge and attitude that those in an organisation possess when it comes to protecting its informational assets must change.

The European Network and Information Security Agency (ENISA) says that "Awareness of the risks and available safeguards is the first line of defence for the security of information systems and networks"[13] and I wholeheartedly agree.

But we can't assume that just making people aware of their role ensures their competence to manage risk. Even if we test someone's awareness of knowledge, there is no certainty that on a day-to-day-basis they will do anything differently. Raising awareness actually means very little if it does nothing to influence behaviour.

That's why, as part of our own SABC™ framework, we consider 'behaviour change' to be the only valid outcome of any 'awareness programme'. Unless, of course, your intention is to transfer the blame for a security incident to an employee, so you can show they've been made aware of their roles and responsibilities but failed to comply.

In 99% of cases, data security breaches result from an individual, or individuals, making the wrong choice or taking an inappropriate action that leaves an organisation's systems at risk and open to exploitation.

The UK's Health and Social Care Information Centre (now NHS Digital) has estimated that 80% to 90% of all paper and electronic data breaches result from human, non-malicious 'bad' behaviour. This includes clicking on unsafe links, sending emails with multiple addresses in the 'to' field, losing storage devices or sharing smart cards with colleagues.

When 250 hackers were quizzed about their techniques at Black Hat 2017, most said it was human weakness they exploited to gain access to sensitive data — 31% said they looked first at privileged accounts, then came email accounts at 27%, then user endpoint at 21%.

Other methods made up the remaining 21% of responses.

Most felt human security breaches were due mostly to 'cyber fatigue'. Constant pressure on employees to follow policy, obey good practice, change passwords frequently and implement software updates, provided them with opportunities.

To combat such problems, most organisations give new employees some formal security awareness training that is periodically topped up. However, what that training includes, when it's delivered, and the effectiveness of its results, vary greatly. And it's not surprising. This is a very old school approach that ignores much of what we know about influencing behaviour. So, 'more of the same' awareness training that only adds to cyber fatigue, hardly seems the optimal response.

Isn't it time to lighten the load by creating security information campaigns that influence behaviour through better design? To focus on why people make choices that expose them to risk, rather than automatically tagging them as the 'weakest link', a label that I'm personally uncomfortable with?

Such negative expressions are unhelpful and potentially damaging in terms of how users perceive themselves and security professionals, and how in turn security professionals see them.

Though attitudes are beginning to shift, there's still widespread acceptance that human error and misjudgement are unfixable flaws. A mindset that inevitably lessens the motivation to try to innovate and find a new approach.

But I don't believe people are a problem that can't be put right. In fact, I believe it's this very human factor, the care and vigilance of staff who use a system that's actually the first line of defence, not the last. Unfortunately, it's usually the missing component in the information security awareness equation.

To some extent that's reflected in the development of the information security sector which, as an industry, has grown from $75.5 billion in 2016 to a predicted worth of $105 billion in 2020. According to the US Bureau of Labor Statistics, the growth rate for information security jobs is also much higher than the average for all other occupations. According to Bureau of Labor Statistics, in the United States the rate of growth for information security jobs will be 37% in the decade from 2012 to 2022[14].

That's being reflected in the expansion of infosec teams, which now have on average just over 30 full-time employees. Many now have a headcount of over 80 with CISOs expecting staff numbers to rise by another 5% in 2018[15].

All positive signs for our sector, of course.

But it's not just how much resource is being allocated, it's also where the resource is going. While Gartner says that the security awareness training market is growing "big time" (admittedly from a relatively low baseline of just $1 billion at the end of 2014), this isn't mirrored by spending on end-user awareness. In 2016 the $3,086 spent per 1,000 IT users, though up from the $2,676 of the previous year[15], was effectively a halving in growth from 30% to 15%.

So, are employees being given the right skills to be effective?

According to The Global Information Security Workforce Study (GISWS) 2017[16], Europe will have a digital security skills gap of 350,000 by 2022. We can draw from this that the skills pool is small… and needs to be seriously expanded.

While employees tend to see technical skills, like cloud computing and security, and a knowledge of governance, risk management and compliance as the key to success, hiring managers now prize an ability to communicate and analytical skills above all else in new hires. Unfortunately, these softer skills tend to be those least valued by job-seekers

As part of a wider research programme, our own survey of security professionals from around the world found that nearly half had already begun using specialist behavioural science skills to develop their information security awareness programmes, though one in eight in our survey didn't know if their organisation was using these kinds of skills.

Such growth however, though to be welcomed, causes problems. There's concern among CISOs that there aren't the skills among their teams to tackle awareness, behaviour and culture. This skills shortage is something highlighted by further research from the Ponemon Institute.

Despite the expansion of infosec, there remains a sense of ineffectiveness. This reflects an industry driven forward by a perpetual flow of technical and technological advances that still fail to bring order to the situation they were designed to control.

Again, in our own Marmalade Box survey, around 50% of respondents felt that information security awareness performance was at best average in their organisation.

This patchy picture will persist until we start taking a

more a holistic approach to information security, until then the human factor will still play second fiddle to other disciplines in the sector.

Of course, no system is totally secure and is only as strong as its weakest link. The reality is that it takes only one breach to compromise a whole system.

Currently, there's too much focus on using technology when the focus should be on people. It's time to look at information security awareness through a new lens.

Chapter Three

"If you think good design is expensive, you should look at the cost of bad design."

Ralf Speth, CEO, Jaguar Land Rover

Everything's a Product ... Including Security

I f security were a product, would you buy it? And if you bought it once, would you buy it again? That's a valid question and one I have asked many in different organisations.

To have any point or purpose, a change programme must not only raise awareness of an issue, but also alter behaviours in ways that are expected, wanted and worthwhile.

Most infosec awareness programmes fail in this ambition. So, if we think of security policies, process and procedures as a product designed to bring about change, then it's defective.

But why exactly does this happen? What's broken in the systems we currently use?

I believe it's because, in an effort to be seen to do something, as an industry we have rushed into developing a product that doesn't bring about the positive security behaviours we need to create. The breaches and issues we see more and more are partially a reflection of that fact. If it were a product, this would be equivalent to selling a half-finished prototype.

So, CISOs and others responsible for the security of data and information, have reached for the wrong tools. Most particularly, they have turned to technology to find a magic bullet. However, there is no magic bullet, and in fact technology isn't the right place to look for the answer.

If it can be made by people, it can be broken by people, so why aren't we turning to people for the solution?

When, in a survey, the Ponemon Institute asked CISOs what was top of their threat list, what did they say?

Not technology. Not hackers. Not malware.

But people.

For many CISOs, the 'human factor' is their over-riding concern and yet, as an industry, we still tend to treat weaknesses in information security awareness as a *technology* problem.

This may be the natural reaction, but as a result, infosec campaigns are created and imposed without reference to those whose behaviours we want to change. Security may matter to infosec professionals, but some-times to colleagues in other departments, our infosec initiatives may appear as unwelcome intrusions that slow them down and get in the way of their work.

Few are ever convinced of their merits, since employees simply don't appreciate the complexities of information security or recognise its benefits at any meaningful personal level. So, if we don't attempt to build an appreciation of infosec's value in the first place, we shouldn't be surprised when our shiny new initiatives fail.

Of course, getting buy-in for any change programme is difficult at the best of times. But it's even more so when the relationship between organisation and employee is in flux and sometimes breaking down.

Overwhelmed by stress and disgruntled by how little they are valued, the number of American employees voluntarily quitting[17] their jobs is on the up.

Nearly one in three of us[18] already mistrust our employer, echoing an increasing wave of suspicion, scepticism and doubt that's washing through society.

While fewer than 30% of millennials (those born between 1980 and the mid-1990s) say they are committed to their current job, 60% freely admit they are open to new work opportunities[19]. Their attitudes will change the workplace even faster as they come to outnumber baby boomers and Gen Xers in the workplace[20].

When someone now in their early twenties can expect to have 15 to 20 different jobs in a lifetime, we have entered the age of the 'low engagement employee' who is much less willing to accept what they see as unnecessary or irrelevant to them.

Employees also now bring to the workplace the 'consumer culture' they enjoy outside it. So, they value and expect greater choice, a quality 'user experience', input into decision making and expect to benefit from products and services tailored to their needs.

On top of this, there's the steady progression towards the 'remote first workplace'. In the UK, Office of National Statistics data shows that 4.2 million people were working from home in 2015. In many metropolitan areas of the United States, telecommuting tops public transportation as the commute option of choice.

With location and attendance no longer essential requirements for employment, that's created a growing number of independent consultants, contractors and freelancers disconnected from the restrictions and disciplines of the traditional office ... and that includes infosec protocols.

None of this creates an environment in which you can simply 'rebadge' a tired and previously tried security awareness product and expect it to make any real difference when it comes to changing behaviour. Knowing what you should do differently means nothing, if you persist in doing what you have always done.

"If you always do what you've always done, you'll always get what you've always got."

Henry Ford

Instead, we need to redesign our campaigns and initiatives, so they better meet the needs of our 'consumers', the end users whose behaviour we are trying so hard to influence.

In the words of commentator and digital entrepreneur Seth Godin: "Don't find customers for your products, find products for your customers."

Of course, human nature is such that if you try to change another's behaviour they naturally resist. That's because they value their perceived freedom of choice and so feel pressured and trapped when things are imposed. Austrian psychiatrist and Holocaust survivor Viktor Frankl talks of the space between stimulus and response where we have a power of choice, and that makes us feel free. Today, we talk about this as being 'mindful'.

It means that if you want a programme to bring about behavioural change, you must consider the preferences, attitudes, thoughts, feelings, opinions, beliefs, desires, frustrations, fears and values of your audience. If you don't, there's an inevitable 'friction' that cannot be overcome, and it's this that makes infosec programmes fail.

Our own research and experience reveal a number of sources of such friction.

1. Inadequate skills applied to the problem.

Infosec programmes are often designed and delivered by information security professionals who don't have the optimal mix of non-technical skills required. Unfortunately, without a strong understanding of communication, psychology, training and change management, as we shall see later, it is very difficult to create an infosec programme that employees will buy into.

2. Lack of board level understanding of organisational risk.

There is inadequate communication between the board and the CISO, if there is one in post at all. This means senior executives have a poor or inaccurate understanding of their organisation's risk picture. Consequently, they under-estimate the importance of information security, despite high profile breaches that cost senior executives their jobs. Former chief cyber-strategist at HP Mike Loginov thinks most boards still see cyber-security as a technical or IT issue, and not "a critical business-focused risk".

3. Insufficient organisational support for infosec initiatives.

Without proper C-level support or commitment, infosec programmes aren't taken seriously or given the backing they require or deserve. That means many initiatives are under-funded and lacking in the resources required to implement, manage and administer them effectively. So, though large sums are being allocated to security awareness initiatives, much of it continues to be misspent.

4. Too much focus on ticking boxes

There is an over-reliance on meeting standards and achieving compliance rather than on developing solutions that are aligned with real business risks. As a result, in many organisations security awareness is seen as standalone project rather than something that should be embedded in its DNA and corporate culture.

5. Underwhelming and ineffective content.

The content of infosec programmes is generally poor and ineffective. In reality, an awareness 'programme' may amount to little more than a clause in your contract, some cursory training during an induction day, reviewing and accepting a set of policies, or sitting through a short video presentation.

Sometimes there is computer-based training (CBT), but generally this consists of overly simplistic tick box exercises delivering stale information that's of limited value. In effect, all this proves is that an employee has been informed and can recall for a very short period a correct answer.

This is no guarantee that their behaviour will change in the way that you want.

6. Inadequate measurement practices.

A lack of useful metrics means it's impossible to measure the progress of most infosec initiatives. Often, the sole measure of success is 'how many staff have completed training since the last time?', rather than whether any significant behavioural change has taken place.

Consequently, few, if any, organisations can - hand-on-heart - rate their awareness programmes as 'good', let alone excellent. Demonstrating business benefit of security awareness requires a clearly defined mix of short, medium and long-term metrics.

7. Training that is too infrequent.

Regarding training as a once a year event is no way to embed information or encourage behavioural change. For accurate recall we need to revisit information[21], so what's needed instead is 'spaced repetition' of relevant knowledge. Higher frequency training is especially important when the nature of security threats is changing so fast.

8. A disconnect between security and organisational needs.

Infosec programmes are not sufficiently tailored to an organisation's business or strategic needs. The one-size fits all solutions that are created just aren't effective. No information security awareness programme or behavioural communication campaign takes place in a vacuum, so the unique context or situation always has an impact. This not only shapes the options available but also affects people's behaviour and actions.

9. Complication in preference to simplicity.

Often infosec solutions are overly complicated. As Facebook's one-time Chief Security Officer Alex Stamos has commented that as an industry we are still too "focused on the really sexy difficult problems."[22] He also notes that the security community spends an enormous amount of time and effort on complicated, byzantine vulnerabilities while paying too little attention to the simple, straightforward problems that actually do the bulk of the damage. "We have perfected the art of finding problems over and over again while ignoring the root issues."

10. The human factor.

Finally, and most importantly of course, they also fail to take account of the human factor, which in my experience underpins everything when it comes to information security. The human factor is *the* thing that really can have a transformational effect. So, to close the gap between awareness programmes and behaviour change we need to adopt a new, more customer-centric approach. This means reinventing infosec processes and controls, so they better fit our marketplace and motivate people to move in the right direction.

But moving away from old ways of working will require a significant cultural change in organisations and that's what we're going to look at next.

Chapter Four

"When the culture is strong, you can trust everyone to do the right thing."

Brian Chesky, co-founder and CEO of Airbnb

Creating a New Awareness Culture

Corporate culture is difficult to define precisely. But we can think of it as the accumulation of individuals' behaviours, goals and values. These include those encouraged and tolerated, as well as those that are not.

Culture has also been described as 'how employees think and act when management's not in the room'. In other words, the set of unwritten, unspoken rules that establish the tone and feel of a workplace. Together, these can have a profound effect on any behavioural change programme, such as an information security awareness campaign.

Because organisational culture evolves organically, it is never what you want it to be, but how your customers, suppliers, investors and employees perceive it as being. And once established, corporate culture is difficult to alter. That's all too obvious when companies try to merge.

So, when Daimler, makers of Mercedes-Benz, joined forces with US car firm Chrysler in the late 1990s, it was meant to be a marriage of equals. But irreconcilable differences over company values, pay and operating styles proved obstacles from the start. After suffering major losses, the pair 'split' in 2007, when Daimler sold Chrysler.

In 2000, Time Warner stock was trading at $71.88. Less than 8 years later, it stood at just $15. All due to a failed $350 billion merger with AOL, for which a 'culture clash' was widely blamed.

And when under-performing Hewlett Packard decided it was a good idea to buy fellow strugglers Compaq, many predicted HP's engineering-driven consensus-based culture would be at odds with Compaq's sales focus. They were right. An estimated $13 billion loss in market capitalisation was the price of this doomed relationship.

Cultural incompatibility is why almost a third of all mergers fail, according to America's Society for Human Resource Management (SHRM). So, trying to alter an existing corporate culture to better encompass information security is always going to be a battle. How big that battle will be is in large part down to the way an organisation views and manages risk. That can depend on its sector.

In their book 'Corporate Cultures: The Rites and Rituals of Corporate Life', Terrence Deal and Allan Kennedy classify insurance, medicine and finance as 'low risk' environments, advertising and professional sports as 'macho', while sales-focused organisations have 'work hard, play hard' cultures.

Of course, the most significant factor in creating an organisation's risk culture is likely to be its founder or current CEO. So, their personal appetite for risk may determine the priority given to information security. The risk-averse are much more likely to take infosec seriously and want to create a culture that reflects this.

"The boundaries of any organisation are permeable and usually not particularly clearly defined." [23]

John Traphagan, University of Texas

However, despite what leaders might write in mission statements, memos and directives, it's what we see, feel and experience every day that matters most. Employees quickly learn the 'rules of the game' by seeing who gets hired, fired, promoted and for what. If they see good security behaviours being valued highly, they in turn will start to practise them.

That means team or departmental culture can have a disproportionate effect. With everyone influencing each other, reinforcing departmental norms and resisting change, it's here that attempts to introduce an overarching security culture can derail. In fact, managers who set their own agendas may even take pride in their team being different.

Jeffrey Katzenberg, who turned around Disney's Animation Studio in the 1980s, said: "You've got 90 days to change the culture before it starts changing you." Although he was speaking about change at a corporate level, this aligns with the typical time it takes to change a habit on a personal level[24].

Even if you manage to put a replacement security culture in place, without constant reinforcement employees are likely to revert to what they were doing before. Particularly if small, inconsistent management decisions send mixed messages about the true importance an organisation actually places on information security. So, rather than even using the term 'security culture', we should think instead about 'embedding security values' in the organisational culture.

This may mean even those wanting to become more infosec aware may find it easier to 'go native' and develop less desirable habits than try to sustain a new set of values.

Attempting to create a better information security culture isn't made easier by the fact that many companies still regard infosec as a technical or IT issue and not the critical business-focused risk that it is.

While organisations may say that cyber security is an increasingly high priority for them, one in five businesses and 38% of charities need to update senior managers about such issues, according to the UK Government's latest Cyber Security Breaches Survey[25]. It is given least attention in sectors like construction, entertainment and hospitality.

However, boards can only make intelligent and informed decisions when they are properly engaged and fully understand the potential threats and risk indicators. Failing to keep them adequately informed about cyber security leaves the business vulnerable to things going wrong. Yet the fact that many CISOs still do not report to a member of the board is evidence they don't have the necessary influence at the top table.

More infosec-aware companies are recognising that CISOs now need to sit on the board if they are to better inform the CEO and other executives *before* things go wrong.

Through their input, CISOs can change how executives think about information security. But if they want to influence others effectively, CISOs must learn to be more business-focused, by clearly demonstrating the impact information security awareness has on an organisation's overall success. That means not just using their powers of persuasion to influence relevant audiences but also, when necessary, exhibiting the 'organisational courage' to stand up and challenge business risk decisions that are not good for the company.

To do that, CISOs must be able to speak the language of the board room. This means informing and educating without jargon, avoiding 'scare stories' based on fear, uncertainty and doubt (FUD) and using appropriate metrics that demonstrate the ROI of risk mitigation. Being on the board is also an opportunity for CISOs to learn first-hand what matters to the business and then use this knowledge to adjust the information security strategy accordingly.

CISOs also have a duty to manage executive expectations about what is possible and when. Many in senior management may have unrealistic expectations about how quickly results can be achieved. The "if it's not worked after one week, one month, or one year — it will never work", can be a pervasive and stubborn belief that's hard to eradicate.

Because security awareness is usually compliance-driven, the 6 to 12-month interval between audits tends to establish the duration of any infosec programme. That's not long enough to be effective.

Old behaviours don't change overnight, nor new ones replace them. So, even attempting to embed new attitudes and behaviours in less than two, and more likely three years, simply isn't credible. There are many variables affecting this timeline. Among them are an organisation's cyber security maturity, the specific threat landscape that it faces, the resources being made available to the information security team, the level of senior management support, the quality of the training material being distributed, and capacity to communicate the right message to the right group.

For those looking to bring a structured approach to changing risk culture, John Kotter's 8-Step Process for Leading Change provides a useful framework. One of the steps, removing barriers to action, is a central theme of chapters 4 and 5. Whether you follow Kotter's model or use some other, managing the 'human factor' will always be an implicit component of bringing about change.

But with everyone having their own built-in 'risk thermostat', it seems unreasonable to expect a single all-encompassing initiative to bring about lasting behavioural improvement across an organisation. Yet we mostly create one-size-fits-all awareness campaigns in an attempt to instil a new infosec culture.

Is it even possible to create a separate culture that runs in parallel with a 'corporate' culture? Doesn't everything around us feed into just one overarching culture? If that's the case, and I believe it is, then any attempt to fundamentally change behaviours means shifting a mountain of baggage.

In systems there is an innate tendency always to move towards equilibrium. When equilibrium is lost, the system tries to restore it using feedback loops. In biology this regulating process is called homeostasis. If the same applies in large organisations, any rapid change will conjure up counteracting forces. The bigger the change, the bigger the counteracting force. This creates a no-win situation.

For every action, there is an equal and opposite reaction.

Newton's Third Law

If this is the case, rather than fighting the status quo, maybe we should accept it and instead find ways to lever it to our advantage. If we know how our end users think and behave, we can find ways to influence them to do what is right without resentment, coercion, bullying or bribery.

While not completely dismissing the idea of pursuing a specific infosec culture, I would suggest that rather than trying to impose infosec values on an existing cultural model, recognising disparate culture values and working with them, would be a more effective option. Of course, we can only do that when we clearly understand what these cultural values are in the first place.

So, if we are to achieve this, we must look at redesigning infosec programmes so that 'making the right decision becomes the easiest decision to make'.

And if every department has its own culture, what about that of the infosec department? How is it perceived? Overly technical? Coercive? Non-empathetic? In fact, is the infosec department's very own culture part of the reason that infosec initiatives so often fail?

Infosec is filled with technically minded people, which may make us blind to those who don't share our enthusiasm for technology. We expect others to know what we're talking about and aren't always quick to explain ourselves better when they don't. We use terms and expressions we think commonplace, but which are baffling to those not in the know. And we expect people to quickly do what we think is simple when it isn't to them.

We also assume others also care about what we value when maybe they don't.

But if we are to influence people to do what we want, we need to be able to walk in their shoes for a day, especially given the changing dynamics of the workplace, where many traditional assumptions about how people behave at work no longer hold true. They want to be treated as individuals, don't like being controlled and tend to resist when it comes to towing the corporate line.

On top of this, powerful cultural waves are hitting the workplace from outside. The #MeToo campaign is just one example of how a new cultural paradigm can suddenly appear and have an impact when a tipping point is reached.

But with everyone having their own built-in 'risk thermostat', it seems unreasonable to expect a single comprehensive initiative to lead to lasting behavioural improvement across an organisation. Given the complexity of countless individual attitudes, backgrounds and mindsets, it's day-dreaming to believe that one-size infosec campaigns will work effectively.

We need to become more empathetic — something we are not very good at.

So, if we want others to care about what we value, we need to be in tune with and more empathetic to their values, beliefs and attitudes. To paraphrase the words of digital commentator and entrepreneur Seth Godin, "Don't find customers for your infosec product, find customers for your product".

Perhaps infosec needs to be more chameleon-like, so rather than having its own specific culture it changes colour to suit the needs of each environment within an organisation, identifying and understanding attitudes towards infosec within particular groups and changing its 'colour' accordingly.

If we are to take this much more customer-focused approach, we need to break out of our infosec bubble. One of the best ways to do that is to become more inclusive by introducing people into the mix who do understand what it's like to walk in others' shoes. So, part of the answer to our infosec problem is diversity.

Chapter Five

"Diversity is the art of thinking independently together."

Malcolm Forbes, Entrepreneur & Publisher

Creating Diversity

Organisations become vulnerable when they lack diversity. If you always hire people of similar backgrounds, genders, skillsets and ages, you end up with a limited perspective. That blinkers organisational mindsets and leaves them unable to recognise potential new threats or situations arising.

Diversity on the other hand, leads to alternative, innovative and divergent thought. Working with people who are different from you forces you to think differently yourself. Exactly what is needed in a fast-changing-threat landscape.

Within organisations, research shows that non-homogenous teams are also smarter[26], more willing to re-examine facts, to remain objective and to recognise the biases that might otherwise blind them.

However, while encouraging greater diversity within infosec is a valid response to future uncertainty, unfortunately the infosec community remains predominantly white and male.

US Bureau of Labor Statistics (BLS) show[27] that

among information security analysts just three per cent are Black or African-Americans. According to the International Information System Security Certification Consortium (ISC)², women still only represent 10% of the information security workforce[28], a percentage that hasn't changed for two years.

Even companies such as Google, Facebook and Apple[29], all of whom would consider themselves forward-thinking employers, have come under scrutiny for lack of workforce diversity.

Reaching out to those who are not traditional infosec material is one way to help bridge a yawning digital skills gap that's getting ever-wider. According to a Global Information Security Workforce Study (GISWS), by 2022 Europe will be 350,000 short of the talent that it needs[30]. Executive Director W Hord Tipton of International Information Systems Security Certification Consortium (ISC)² goes even further, saying that as many as 2 million more need to be drawn into our sector[31].

If we are to even come close to plugging this void, we must start thinking differently about recruitment. One of the central messages of this book is that we need to go beyond simply applying technical sticking plasters to wounds. We need instead to focus much more on the human factor, and that requires us to bring in a much wider range of skills.

"Where all think alike, no one thinks very much."

Walter Lippmann, writer

Many hiring decisions are based on gut feel, personal experience and corporate belief systems. As in most sectors, unless infosec hiring managers make a conscious effort to do otherwise, their natural bias means they will continue to favour those they most readily relate to. In effect, often the whole purpose of the recruitment system is to avoid putting square pegs into round holes.

The desire to keep things the same is built in. As a result, many with potentially interesting and usable abilities exclude themselves because of tightly-written job specs that stipulate irrelevant skills or ask for too much experience. Search algorithms reinforce recruitment stereotypes by ignoring those who don't fit a particular template or have the wrong keywords in their CVs.

On the face of it, recruiting 'people like us' makes absolute sense. Homogenous teams made up of the same kind of people *feel* more effective. There's also an innate belief among managers that the more diverse the team, the greater the prospect of conflict within it. Again, that makes sense. When people are similar they tend to understand each other better, so collaboration is smoother. Anyone added to this mix who doesn't quite fit is naturally expected to be a potentially disruptive and counterproductive influence.

And yet, diverse teams actually produce better outcomes precisely *because* there is friction between members[32]. Bringing people with different perspectives together forces them to overcome their differences and discover ways of working more productively together. Often managers over-estimate the degree of conflict within teams[33] and play it safe. So, without even realising it, teams don't diversify because of overblown fears about the tensions and difficulties that will be released.

Of course, those with IT knowledge, analytical skills and understanding of computer science will always be at the centre when it comes combating information security threats. But we limit ourselves by only looking at those with such backgrounds.

With only a hammer in our toolbox, we tend to treat every problem as a nail. If we continue to recruit carbon copies who think, talk and behave just like those who have gone before, we do ourselves no favours. By ignoring those who are 'different', we become one-trick ponies, and that just constrains our effectiveness.

If we are to appreciate why people make mistakes in the first place, we can only do this by employing those who understand how errors come about and can devise appropriate strategies. That requires a certain empathy, which isn't one of the information security sector's strengths. As Facebook's Chief Security Officer Alex Stamos acknowledged when speaking at Blackhat USA 2017: "We have a real inability to put ourselves in the shoes of the people we are trying to protect."

If people are both the problem and the solution, then it seems somewhat perverse that we should try and solve that problem using only technology. That means we need people who can provide 'human solutions' as well as technical ones.

We need to realise that 'non-standard' employees have skills worth embracing. That means we must start selecting from a far wider range of disciplines. Those with a background in humanities, international relations and foreign languages, for instance, should be chosen *because* of their lack of a technical background, which allows them to come at problems from different angles. We then need to hire and promote people based on these new skillsets, not just the established ones.

Diverse backgrounds are vital, because as Alex

Stamos has also said: "You never know what kind of problems you're going to get and so it's much better to have a toolbox with all different kinds of tools than to only have the best screwdrivers in the world."

**Lack of empathy creates a barrier
that once created is hard to break down.**

In any event, increasing workplace diversity is a good business decision. Consultants McKinsey have found that firms with greater ethnic and racial diversity generate financial returns above their industry average[34]. While companies with more women are more likely to bring new innovations to the market[35].

If infosec is to strengthen and enhance its role within the organisation, it needs to adopt a much more holistic workforce and recruitment approach. That means creating multi-disciplinary teams that comprise more than the usual technical, analytical, risk assessment and incident investigation skills.

That involves seeking out new talent in new places and not doing the rounds of the same careers fairs or running last year's recruitment programme once again. We need to open ourselves up to new applicants and be much more flexible about who we recruit.

In turn this requires us to think again about the nature of our workforce. We can no longer expect people to come to us as the finished product. We need to see them instead as raw material that we can change through apprenticeship opportunities, certification programmes and other training and upskilling.

This, of course, means hiring managers who under-stand and recognise the skills required to operate successfully in a modern environment and not just keep on hiring others like themselves.

For instance, to be able to explain clearly the importance of information security, we need people with strong inter-personal and communication skills. People who can break out of the technical bubble and bridge the knowledge gap that exists not just between us and end users, but also within the board. CISOs must be able to repurpose their usual terminology so that it resonates in new, commercially-focused ways. In fact, a CISO's greatest asset will be their ability to match information security objectives to a CEO's needs. This means recognising the unique perceptions of each executive and creating pathways to understanding that will enable them, individually and collectively, to make better informed decisions.

They must also be able to build relationships and develop the authority to influence others to win the backing of the executive team. As well as this, they must have credible expertise in both business and infosec matters.

We should also encourage those with technical skills to prize 'softer' skills as part of their career development. That will enable them to better appreciate any behavioural initiatives developed by others in their team.

Fortunately, there are signs that infosec is beginning to embrace this message. As part of a wider research programme, our own worldwide survey of security professionals found that nearly half had already begun using specialist behavioural science skills to develop their information security awareness programmes. However, one in eight in our survey didn't know if their organisation was using those kinds of skills.

To identify some of the skills we need, infosec would do well to look at the world of marketing, particularly those involved in selling online. Every day, e-commerce firms succeed or fail through their ability to build relationships with and influence strangers. That requires them to continually adjust, change and rethink what they do so that it moves ever closer to what the market wants. If they don't make a sale they understand it's not because there's something wrong with their customer, but because it's either the wrong product or they haven't promoted it properly.

Instead of seeing failure to comply as solely the user's fault, we should see it as being down to us because we have 'sold' them the wrong infosec product in the first place! So, if we want to create more effective infosec programmes, we should remember the words of management consultant Peter Drucker, who said: "The aim of marketing is to make selling superfluous". In other words, we need to create the best fit infosec product for our market, rather simply defaulting to a 'take it or leave it' approach.

If we start to think more like marketeers, we will be in a much better position to design more effective information security programmes.

Chapter Six

"Everything should be made as simple as possible, but not simpler."

Albert Einstein

Better Behaviour By Design

The human brain is immensely complex and powerful. Yet, though it's capable of incredible feats, we don't like to use it more than we have to. Given the choice, we opt for least mental effort. So, when we can, we tend to go for not what's most rewarding, but what's easiest.

To do this, we use what psychologist Daniel Kahneman calls *fast* thinking. This is the intuitive, instant and unconscious system we default to in preference to the *slow* alternative. We reserve this for more rational, conscious, reflective reasoning. Exactly what's needed for analysing situations, solving complex problems and making major decisions.

Given that our 'fast' automatic thinking system takes precedence, it's hardly surprising that in a pressurised workplace, where competition for our attention is relentless, our factual, logical infosec campaigns don't engage.

When interruptions continually punctuate the day — we spend almost one-third of our time managing the 94 business emails we receive every day[36] — who wants to plough through yet more information security awareness material? It's an unwanted, unwelcome distraction that we don't have the energy for. No wonder many of us bypass or ignore rules and regulations we consider unreasonable or of limited value.

So, when infosec campaigns fail, it's generally not through deliberate ill-will, but because we aren't using the same mental models as our audience. Yet we assume employees must or will do what we want them to do.

However, if we knew what these models were, we would be much better equipped to design strategies that actually worked. That means recognising the way our brains work and redesigning our infosec campaigns accordingly, based on a greater understanding of the mechanisms of the mind.

If we can bring the two together, we will become much more effective 'choice architects' who create situations in which people will naturally make better decisions about information security.

That requires us to let go of previous mindsets about people being an unmanageable problem when it comes to information security. We can't simply repeat what we've done in the past and expect a different result. If what we currently do isn't working, we shouldn't be afraid to think differently.

Unfortunately, most CISOs are under pressure and look for rapid solutions. So, they tend to reach for the same familiar tools rather than ones that actually remove the barriers preventing compliance.

And every one of these barriers left in place, large, small, real or imagined, is a point of friction that can derail any infosec initiative by hindering behavioural change.

If all stakeholders are not brought on board, they can sabotage infosec efforts unintentionally, though sometimes deliberately, when under pressure to deliver their own different goals. If, for them, infosec implementation is being done on a 'best endeavour' basis, we shouldn't necessarily expect their unswerving support.

The answer to this, of course, is to make changes in infosec awareness, behaviour and culture a measured deliverable that will positively affect their performance.

The business itself can also prove an unexpected hurdle through its own actions, if these are contrary to improving infosec best practice. When training people to recognise phishing attacks, for example, you shouldn't be sending what could be construed as dubious emails at the same time. It shouldn't happen, but it does.

I've already mentioned the lack of skills and experience, not just within the infosec team but throughout the organisation, as another obstacle to creating significant behavioural change. If you have limited in-house capabilities, you are more likely to stick with the same tired, ineffective solutions rather than explore new ways of working.

The most obvious challenge, of course, is how to actually encourage behavioural change among the largely uninterested audience on the 'shop floor'.

The awareness we traditionally look to instil may create temporary knowledge, but whether behaviours alter in line with that knowledge is always uncertain and open to debate.

The reality is that you can never push knowledge into someone's brain. They must pull it in themselves. That only happens when they accept the value of what you are offering and are willing to do it because it causes them minimal 'pain'.

"When a behaviour is easier to do, it is more likely people will do it."

Nir Eyal, author of 'Hooked'

In other words, how much energy, time and effort someone 'thinks' they will have to expend determines their willingness to do something. Anything we *perceive* as difficult or time-consuming, we procrastinate about and put off doing. Even small, easy tasks don't get tackled if they are mistakenly thought of as problematic.

So, if you want to encourage compliance, always 'make the right behaviour the easiest behaviour' by reducing the perceived 'transaction cost' involved in any infosec activity.

Unfortunately, we often keep transaction costs too high because we tend to see information security awareness as a complex problem requiring a complex solution. Rather than flattening out the 'speed bumps' that are obstacles to behavioural change, we simply create more. So, we constantly overload employees, for example, with too much information too soon. Miller's Law states that the limits of our short-term memory mean we can only keep around seven bits of data in our head at once, yet we persist in sending out mountains of infosec material.

Rather than flooding people with data, we should be delivering smaller, more digestible units of information that users can absorb much more easily. Controlling information flow is particularly important for 'new starters' who, unlike more established employees, have no existing foundation skills or knowledge in their long-term memory to call upon, other than what they have brought with them from previous jobs or roles.

When older knowledge interferes with the brain's ability to accept new information, learning doesn't always happen quickly or easily.

High-frequency, small-chunk awareness programmes are much more effective than intense once-a-year training that is easily forgotten and provides no regular opportunity to reinforce new behaviours. With cyber threats evolving daily, this also helps employees to stay better informed and ensures their risk detection skills remain up-to-date and relevant.

As well as cutting the transaction cost of individual infosec tasks, this progressive disclosure of information creates a sense of moving forward among end users. It's also a much more pragmatic training solution, given that on average an employee can devote only 1% of their working time towards learning new things[37]. That's just 4 minutes 48 seconds a day!

If you want to make the right behaviour the easiest behaviour, you must remove ambiguity and confusion. Every moment someone spends thinking about what they should do increases the physical, mental and emotional transaction cost. When this becomes too great, we can end up making poor infosec decisions based on impulse, gut instinct and our many cognitive biases, which I talk about in the next chapter.

On the other hand, when people know exactly what's expected of them, they are more likely to comply. So, give staff a clear, unambiguous infosec plan to follow, with every step accurately detailed, clearly articulated and all the information they need readily available. They will be much more willing to behave in the way you want.

So, simple processes and tools that ensure staff know what to do next help reduce the transaction costs of infosec actions. For instance, by using 'if-this-then-that' planning to trigger an action in response to an event, we take out the 'the think component' from a situation and so cut the cognitive load.

Checklists do the same. These are widely used in areas like medicine, where mistakes can have even more catastrophic effects than in information security. In his book, The Checklist Manifesto[38], surgeon Atul Gawande reveals how implementing simple checklists can slash medical error rates without the need for technology.

One sure way to add to the mental effort required to reach a decision is to give people too many choices. We tend to think that more options must be better than fewer, but in reality, this often leads instead to cognitive exhaustion.

Not only does it make choosing a longer process (Hick's Law), but it can also leave us paralysed through indecision, what psychologist Barry Schwartz describes as the 'paradox of choice'.

> *"We all assume in modern western societies that since choice is good, more choice must be better … that turns out not to be true."*

Barry Schwartz, psychologist

So, instead of being liberated by being able to select from alternatives, the opposite is true.

By the end of each day, it's been said that we've made around 35,000 decisions[39]. Even ignoring information is a choice. That means it's easy for anyone to feel overwhelmed.

The more choices we must make, the more tired our brains becomes. And when a brain starts running 'on empty' it looks to conserve energy. Then short-term gains rather than long-term effort become the priority. When that happens, we are much more likely to respond impulsively and so make the wrong choices. We should therefore do all we can not to add to people's emotional and mental burden by making sure that infosec information is communicated in a highly targeted and focused way.

So, the more infosec decisions we can remove, automate or make less demanding the greater will be the compliance effect because you reduce the mental effort involved. That means going through every infosec process in detail, eliminating all unnecessary steps and ensuring that the right behaviour becomes the easiest behaviour — and the default position.

When creating any infosec awareness campaign, we have to remember we aren't the end user. That means we must keep others' background, experience and skills in mind and never assume they will think or behave the way we would in any specific situation. You may believe protecting a computer's data from cyber threat is important but asking a technical novice to choose a sufficiently random password, store it securely, recollect it when required then input it correctly is to put a significant cognitive burden on them when they have so many other things to do.

Neither can you presume that others know how to do something. That's because they may actually know surprisingly little, or because of the 'curse of confidence' that leads them to over-estimate their own abilities. Nearly two-thirds of passwords are forgotten within three months, according to Joseph T. Hallinan in his book 'Why We Make Mistakes', probably because most people mistakenly believe they will remember them.

So, perhaps one of the most effective ways to reduce the transaction cost of initiatives is for us to learn from our customers. How can they help us? Why don't they do what we want them to do? Why do they find the infosec tasks we give them so hard? Why don't they comply? What stops them from engaging?

The more we understand why others are reluctant, unwilling or hesitate to do what we want them to do, the better able we are to construct more effective infosec programmes.

Consider how much resource, time and effort you currently spend pushing out communications compared with how much is spent listening to what our audience has to say. But shift from 'broadcast' to 'conversation' and you immediately increase engagement.

Seeking the contribution of others may require us to park our egos, but it would seem to me to be an obvious way to develop more effective infosec policies, and it shouldn't be that hard to do.

Employees wrote the handbook of project management software firm Basecamp[40], which among other things details the firm's security policies. And because it wasn't forced on them from above but organically developed, you can imagine how that might change the way it works and reads.

If we are intent on minimising the transaction cost of change, then one of the best things we can do is recognise that creating behavioural change is essentially an evolutionary process.

Trying to force the pace, which we do when we impose, only leads to resistance and less compliance among employees who are uncomfortable with 'the shock of the new'. Often the better option is to move forward incrementally rather than going for big breakthroughs that are not only harder to initiate, but also less sustainable long-term.

In software development, this type of 'hacking' is not a risk but a creative process that applies the lessons learned from previous iterations to create a better product. Each improvement, though inconsequential in itself, adds up to create significant change. This is the concept of marginal gains.

A well -known example of marginal gains in practice is that of Britain's national cycling team, who two decades ago were considered also-rans in the cycling world. One commentator even called them 'a laughing stock'.

But through a combination of lottery funding and the magic of marginal gains, Team GB won 7 of Great Britain's 29 gold medals in the 2012 Olympic Games. Chris Hoy, Mark Cavendish and Victoria Pendleton became household names in the process. That same year, Bradley Wiggins became the first British winner of the Tour de France. Another British rider, Chris Froome, went on to win the same race in three of the four subsequent years. Suddenly, Britain was the planet's hottest cycling nation, in large part because it had made tiny 1% improvements in as many areas as possible. Infosec should start doing the same by seeing each weakness not as a threat, but an opportunity for improvement in policies, processes and procedures.

> *"If you broke down everything you could think of that goes into riding a bike, and then improved it by one percent, you will get a significant increase when you put them all together."*
>
> Sir Dave Brailsford, British Cycling's one-time performance director

As well as minute attention being paid to training regimes, nutrition and equipment, the team sought marginal gains wherever they could. So, when dirt and dust affected bike maintenance, workshop floors were painted white to make it easier to spot. New hand washing techniques were introduced to cut down on infections. And pillows were tested for comfort, so riders could enjoy the best night's sleep.

In effect, this was 'kaizen' — the Japanese doctrine of continuous improvement — applied to sport. In our industry, we might think of it as a "Plan-Do-Check-Act" sequence. You may recognise similar principles contained in ISO27001 and other internationally recognised security standards.

The difference achieved through each marginal gain may appear inconsequential when viewed individually, but it's the sum of them all that makes for such an incredibly powerful process, which is why we have made them very much part of our proprietary SABC™ framework.

Because the transaction cost is much lower with smaller tasks, people are more willing and motivated to do them. And as Robert Cialdini explains in his book 'Influence', if we can get people commit to a goal, however small, they are much more likely to deliver that goal. We are then in a position to generate a domino effect, with one new behaviour leading to a cascade of others.

To use the words of Stanford professor and 'habit specialist' BJ Fogg, "You can never change just one behaviour. Our behaviours are interconnected, so when you change one behaviour, other behaviours also shift."

If we can get people moving in this way, we are much less likely to require the usual corporate response to uncooperative employees: adopting a 'do it or else' approach or offering incentives. iPads seem popular at the moment.

Using extrinsic motivation like this, as some organisations do, may work in the short-term, but it isn't the answer to achieving long-term behavioural change when it comes to infosec. In fact, studies show this approach can actually make behaviour worse because the reward is turned into a tool and the behaviour merely a means to an end. Instead, we need to encourage our audience's intrinsic motivations, so they do things because they *want* to.

**When it comes to incentives,
"pay enough or don't pay at all."**

Training and development have a positive impact on employee engagement. So, as employees develop professionally and learn new skills, they become invested in the company, which improves productivity and profitability. Helping someone achieve mastery is one of the greatest ways to reward people, encourage engagement to bring about longer-term change.

But even giving people the perception of control is sufficient. Being able to make choices about the inconsequential creates a sense of ownership that's sufficiently motivational to get things done. This is the reason placebo buttons are put on pedestrian crossings and lifts. They serve no real function other than make us feel we have some control over an automated system. It's why Instagram always shows it's working even when it's not connected to the internet. It's why progress bars we see when downloading content make us feel as though something's happening, even though they bear no relationship to the amount of data received.

Whatever we do, risk mitigation is all about reducing the set of circumstances under which something can happen and that has to be seen against the backdrop of the volatile and fast-changing nature of society, business and the workplace.

There is no getting away from it, we are by nature flawed and inconsistent creatures, more suited to pursuing novelty and excitement than detail and discipline.

That's why, to design more effective infosec systems, we need to think … irrationally.

Chapter Seven

"We can be blind to the obvious, and we are also blind to our blindness."

Daniel Kahneman

Changing Behaviour Without Changing Minds

I n the 1970s, psychologists Daniel Kahneman and Amos Tversky introduced the world to *cognitive biases*. These are thinking shortcuts we apply unconsciously to different situations when making choices.

They're not occasional mental aberrations, but systemic thinking patterns we follow repeatedly and cannot control. Together, they filter information on our behalf without our consent, every one of them colouring the way we look at the world, whether we're at work or at home. It's to our set of cognitive biases we default when under pressure and have neither the time nor the inclination for 'deep thought'.

We've already seen how our fast thinking system is our system of choice. So, rather than rationally identifying and researching all our options, then weighing up the pros and cons of each before choosing the 'best' solution, we make rash decisions based on inadequate information, misguided thinking and ill-informed knowledge.

Kahneman and Tversky's 'behavioural' approach to

economic decision-making flies in the face of two centuries of traditional economic rationality. This assumed we would always try to gain the greatest benefit for ourselves when given the chance. As Adam Smith, the father of economics, wrote in The Wealth of Nations nearly two and a half centuries ago: "It is not from the benevolence of the butcher, the brewer, or the baker that we expect our dinner, but from their regard to their own interest."

When we have more information than ever to help us make the right decision, this way of thinking seems counter to logic. But paradoxically, in a complex world where we can't accurately calculate risk and probability, our cognitive biases, illogical though they may seem, tend to work in our favour.

By using these mental shortcuts, we can cut through the 'white noise' of often contradictory information to focus on just a few key factors that matter to us. When we're weighed down by cognitive load, this not only saves us time but can actually lead us to make better decisions.

This helps to explain why appealing solely to logic using facts and figures often fails as a strategy and can actually reinforce already entrenched attitudes. So, while we may use rationality as our weapon of choice, it generally won't win us the war. Research shows that if evidence undermines or contradicts someone's ideas or beliefs, they will find reasons to ignore or reject it. Anyone who has challenged someone's world view will have experienced the 'backfire effect'[41] as they become increasingly immovable.

And once someone has ignored or rejected your ideas, you can't bring them on board merely by repeating what you've already said. Trying to bludgeon your audience into submission by giving them the same old material just will not work. Rather than trying to change behaviour through rational argument, often we are better off doing nothing.

Unfortunately, most infosec campaigns and transformation programmes do try to convince through repeated rational argument, when what is actually required is a more 'emotional' human engagement that takes into account those cognitive biases.

This allows us to gently 'nudge' people into adopting new behaviours and making 'better' choices almost effortlessly. The best nudges make it easy to adopt one behaviour over another because we are innately hard-wired to follow the line of least resistance and take the easiest option. As we saw in the previous chapter, often it's the transaction cost of doing something differently that stops us from taking a particular course of action.

Nobel Prize winning behavioural scientist Richard Thaler, a leading nudge proponent, tells the story of a school that wanted to encourage pupils to eat better. Rather than banning sugary sweets or subsidising salads, the head teacher simply put the healthier foods at eye level in the school canteen, making it easier for children to choose carrot sticks over French fries.

It's by learning from disciplines such as behavioural economics that I believe we can significantly improve the effectiveness of our infosec campaigns.

"When we think wrongly, we do so predictably."

Dan Ariely, behavioural psychologist

In one of my Rethinking the Human Factor podcast episodes[42], Dan Ariely, who has been voted one of the world's most influential psychologists, gives another example of how behavioural economics can help change people's motivation.

When a US online pharmacy wanted to switch customers from expensive brands to cheaper generic products, they created an amazing deal to incentivise the change — those who made the switch would pay nothing for their medication for a year. Yet fewer than 10% took up the offer.

Why did customers reject this 'no brainer' option that would have saved them hundreds of dollars a year?

Because the transaction cost — though very small — was still too high for them to act. On the other hand, the default response – doing nothing – was frictionless and therefore the much easier option.

The 'best' behavioural science solution would have been to make receiving the generic medicine the default choice. But since this would have been illegal, instead the pharmacy *made everyone re-register,* giving them the option to switch away from branded medication at the same time. Yet more evidence that we do things that take least effort, or we don't do them at all.

So, by using our knowledge of cognitive biases to create lines of least resistance[43], we have the potential to put in place new infosec behaviours that over time become embedded as habits we default to.

That means we should always be aware of how cognitive biases creeping into decision-making can affect infosec behaviours for better and worse.

There's no agreement about exactly how many

cognitive biases exist, though this codex of cognitive biases lists over 180.

To get a deeper insight into the wide range of biases, Rolf Dobelli's book 'The Art of Thinking Clearly' is a great starting point. These are just a few to consider when designing an infosec awareness campaign.

Loss Aversion. We hate losing and do all we can to avoid it, even if it's something we never wanted or had an interest in previously. To convince someone to do something, rather than focusing on the advantages, highlight how it will help them avoid the *dis*advantages. The fear of loss motivates people more.

Status Quo Bias. We only change behaviour when the incentive to do so is sufficiently strong; otherwise, we tend to stick with what we know. If you ask your audience to make too many decisions at once, they are more likely to feel overwhelmed, confused and reject every choice you offer.

Anchoring. What people see first creates a powerful 'anchor' that affects their subsequent thinking. Present the wrong information at the wrong time and you create a mental roadblock that's hard to overcome. Retailers present the most expensive item first, so others seem cheap in comparison. How to use this cognitive bias? Think carefully about your communication sequence.

Bandwagon effect. The probability one person will change their behaviour increases depending on the number of people they see with that behaviour. That's why using social proof is such a powerful technique because it reassures by showing that others are already exhibiting a desired behaviour. That's why providing 'social proof' is such a powerful technique, as what see or think others are doing greatly influences our own behaviour. So, for example, simple benchmarking statistics that revealed to doctors whether they were prescribing more or less than their peers substantially reduced unnecessary antibiotic prescriptions[44]. Could we use something similar in infosec by creating short training modules that use real-life scenarios and characters employees can identify with are more likely to relate to?

Confirmation bias. We are much more likely to believe information that confirms our existing opinions, so we seek it out. For example, when people are presented with evidence that run counter to their political beliefs their brains 'light up' as though they are suffering physical pain[45]. That really shows none of us like to be proven wrong.

Using powerful cognitive biases to bring about behavioural change makes some feel uneasy. And when used to manipulate someone to their disadvantage you can see why. We all know the feeling of discomfort when someone tries to make us do something we wouldn't otherwise do. Cab firm Uber, for instance, has been heavily criticised for using cognitive biases[46] to encourage drivers to work longer hours using a technique that induces a mental state called the 'ludic loop' by pushing them towards a goal they can never quite reach.

We need to be mindful that when we design information security awareness programmes or communication campaigns we never do so in a vacuum. So, how we respond in any situation is intimately connected to our own individual preferences and inclinations, and what gives us pleasure or pain. Context and environment have an impact.

In Drunk Tank Pink Adam Alter writes about how small changes in our environment affect behaviour. As he says: "There isn't a single version of 'you.' When you're surrounded by litter, you're more likely to be a litterbug; when you're walking past buildings with broken windows, you're more likely to disrespect the property that surrounds you. These norms change from minute to minute …"

If we want to create a better choice environment in which people find it easier to do the right thing, then we need to start thinking differently. We need to shift the focus away from trying to educate through facts and information and to look instead at how cognitive biases can lead us to a more holistic approach that brings about change in a way that's much more consistent with our usual behaviours.

And with over 40% of our daily actions[47] said to be down to habit, if we can get people operating in infosec autopilot, then we are a long way down the road to solving our risk awareness issues.

When good infosec practice becomes a habit, people have to think less intensively and so focus their mental energy elsewhere

But leaving old habits behind and replacing them

with new ones isn't easy. That's why nearly everyone who tries to lose weight gains back the pounds in less than two years. No wonder instilling infosec best practice is a challenge.

But by tapping into the power of cognitive biases, if we can get someone to do just one thing differently, then we have successfully persuaded them, despite what they continue to think or believe. And this is an important point, because it's easy to assume that to change someone's infosec behaviour we might have to change what they believe before they will do it. Fortunately, that's not the case, in fact, quite the reverse.

Trying to get someone to change a belief is notoriously difficult. Just picture someone you know with very strong beliefs and you can see why.

But if you can get someone to *behave* in a new way first, often their attitudes and beliefs will change as a result. So powerful is this causation effect, that if we do something that's in conflict with a belief, we generally tend to modify what we believe rather than change the behaviour. This is why people can still hold onto old attitudes even when logically they should no longer apply.

That means, if you can get end users to act in a more risk-aware way, they are much likely to come to believe that they are risk aware individuals in reality. With that new attitude in place, we enter a virtuous circle as they become increasingly willing to adopt ever more habitual infosec behaviours.

Of course, one of the greatest barriers to breaking old habits is unlearning what we already know. If this contradicts the fresh material, we are particularly likely to dismiss it. A process psychologists call proactive interference.

That means we have to find ways to present new infosec information in ways that undermine the "coherence"[48] of someone's current views. That comes down very much to effective communication, something I look at in the next chapter.

Chapter Eight

"How well we communicate is determined not by how well we say things, but how well we are understood."

Andrew Grove, co-founder & CEO, Intel

Managing the Message

Psychological insights from disciplines like behavioural economics can help us design more effective infosec initiatives. But there's no point to policies, procedures and processes if no one knows they exist, understands what they mean, or is persuaded by what they say. In other words, if we want to bring about long-term behavioural change, we need to understand the importance of communication.

Unfortunately, persuasive communication is often a missing component from infosec awareness campaigns. As a result, core messages are ignored, old habits don't change and the impact of even the best security initiatives is diminished.

When we fail to communicate, or worse still we miscommunicate, we create further barriers that stop our audience from understanding the value of information security. As behavioural economist Dan Ariely explained in one of my Rethinking the Human Factor podcast episodes[42], you can't expect people to do what you want them to do if they don't appreciate what's on offer.

Effective communication is critically important when attempting to create any behavioural change, particularly when there's indifference or even antipathy to what's being suggested.

So, we need to think much more carefully about how to move communication from being simply a 'telling' tool to one that influences and persuades. If I don't understand why something matters, then it certainly won't matter to me. For instance, many people don't appreciate how easy it is for algorithms to 'guess' passwords. Consequently, they think they are choosing secure passwords when they're not.

Unfortunately, most corporate communication is governed by guidelines that strip away the soul from the message. The resulting lifeless, passive and 'arms-length' announcements, appeals or exhortations don't resonate with the audience, let alone change hearts and minds.

In an attempt to cover all the bases, we often over-communicate, confusing quantity with quality, rather than focusing on what actually matters. We bombard end users with volumes of detail they don't care about and can't absorb. Overwhelmed by 'content shock', it's no wonder they either switch off entirely or focus on the bits of information they consider most relevant, ignoring everything else. Simply delivering more of the same, rather than helping us make better decisions, leads us to make poorer ones.

"Persuasion skills exert a far greater influence over others' behaviours than formal power structure do."

Robert Cialdini, author of 'Influence, the Psychology of Persuasion.'

In some risk-averse sectors, like financial services, overly legalistic security policies make for particularly heavy reading. Lawyers generally resist moves towards simpler language, arguing that such obscure words are necessary because they have been tested in court. In fact, the reverse is more likely. Wording that's unclear probably *hasn't* been scrutinised in court, as judges usually penalise those who use language with obscure meaning.

Ineffective communication is another consequence of regarding information security as a technical issue. That has left us short of trained communicators and once again underlines the importance of bringing a range of skills into the infosec sector or improving what we've already . If we don't, we will continually default to the easiest solution: presenting generic, one-size-fits-all content that doesn't bring about behavioural change.

For our infosec initiatives to have maximum impact, we must create content that's much more tailored to individual needs and overcomes the barriers that stop the right behaviour becoming the easiest behaviour. Those familiar with Neuro-Linguistic Programming (NLP) will be aware that we all have different learning styles and that knowing someone's personal preference can have a profound impact on how that they take in new material.

That means presenting information in whatever way is easiest for each of our audiences to understand and use. So, those who are comfortable and competent with numbers will respond better to statistics, facts and figures. While those who like to 'see' things will appreciate a much more visual approach.

So, when looking to change someone's behaviour learn how they make choices first[49] *before* trying to influence them with data. Simply attempting to guess or generalise about what these 'decision drivers' might be is likely to lead us astray. This requires us to think a little more 'psychologically' and to move away from merely trying to convince people through logic, argument and data.

Risk-based education and awareness campaigns that target those with access to critical systems and sensitive business data, or who have shown themselves insufficiently risk averse through incidents and failed assessments, are steps towards more tailored infosec content.

But we need to do much more if we want to engage with our audience. We need to improve our messaging by making infosec communications less formal and more conversational. No piece of infosec communication should ever read like a list of demands.

It also means creating a tone of voice for our communications. Tone of voice is about capturing and conveying through words an organisation's personality and values. We should take tone of voice seriously because if what we say doesn't 'sound' right to our audience, they will be disinclined to engage or will feel misunderstood.

Does your infosec department have a tone of voice? Almost certainly. Though it's probably developed by default and not been deliberately created with your audience in mind. If so, the personality that comes across is most likely technical, detailed and somewhat coercive, based on achieving compliance through 'fear'.

If you would like to know more about tone of voice, there's an interesting podcast I've done with Ben Afia, an expert in making communications more human[50].

Earlier in the book I talk about how the decisions we make aren't rational, but based on a complex mix of cognitive bias, emotion and personal experience. Consequently, arguments made using facts and figures often don't engage, even in the 'logical' work environment. That's why many organisations are turning to stories to better express a message. So much so, that storytelling has become one of the hot trends in PR[51].

Stories work because they engage our brains at a deeper level and in ways that not only spark interest but also persuade and inspire action much more than logic ever can. If your story is strong enough, it will trigger an emotional response that the reader remembers longer. By changing the context, stories help us think differently about information. You can use stories to present an infosec message in its entirety, to illustrate through example, or to create mental images.

This is why I created 'The Analogies Project', an online library of analogies, metaphors and stories security professionals can use to better communicate an infosec message by relating it to everyday and historic events and situations.

Single words can matter.
The mere use of the word "because"
triggers a powerful compliance reaction

Stories speak to our hearts. When we read or hear a story, seven areas of our brains simultaneously activate, triggering emotions and bringing into play senses like touch, taste and even smell. If you read the word 'lavender' in a story[52], you can actually smell it.

Does an attempt to create emotion work in a commercial environment? Very much so. In a six-year-long study, customer experience firm Beyond Philosophy found that those in B2B sectors tended to rely on their opinions and emotions more than ordinary 'customers'.

Don't be afraid to make your communications more human because, in our digital age, that is valued more than ever.

Stories can also encourage behavioural change by providing social proof that others are already behaving in a particular way. We are naturally inclined to be part of a crowd. So, if we see others behaving in a way we consider to be the social norm, we are much more likely to do what they do, as we don't want to feel excluded or stand out. In fact, conforming is such a powerful 'hot button' that we will do the wrong thing rather than go against the flow.

While content and tone of voice are the 'big rocks' of communication, there are many small things we can do to tweak our infosec message to give it more persuasive power. And as we learn more and more from neuro-science about how the brain works, increasingly we come to realise that even seemingly insignificant changes have a much greater impact than we once thought. In communication, small things really do matter.

As an example, let's consider the world of e-commerce for a moment. This is a sector where companies, many of them amongst the world's largest, continually have to find better ways to persuade potential buyers through one primary interface … their website.

Because a digital interface like this lacks micro-emotions[53] – the small visual cues we get from a person's facial expressions and body language - these companies have become adept at 'nuancing' every part of a site, down to the smallest components, so they squeeze the most from it.

Through continuous split testing[54] of many variables, they can see what works and what doesn't, then adjust accordingly. Take typefaces.

You've probably given little thought to the one you use for infosec communications. It may well be just the corporate font defined by a branding agency. But whether you use Arial, Helvetica, Cambria or Calibri, the lines and curves of each character have an impact by affecting the reader's mood and behaviour in what Microsoft psychologist Kevin Larson calls the 'aesthetics of reading'[55]. So, for example, if you read about an exercise programme in a less legible font, you will rate it harder than if you read about it in a clearer typeface[56].

Whether a typeface is serif or not also has an effect. We think we read faster and comprehend more when a serif font is used. And studies show text in the serif font Georgia is easier and 8% faster to read than a sans serif typeface like Helvetica[57]. Perhaps it should be the go-to font for infosec comms?

Larger font sizes also produce a stronger emotional response[58] in readers. Perhaps because most of us lose visual acuity over time, a larger font causes less frustration and so makes us more willing to comply with requests. If you have a higher ratio of older employees to younger digital natives in your workforce, adjusting font size could make a perceptible difference.

My point here is not to add to the debate over the best typeface to use if you want to persuade and influence others, but to emphasise that in communication small things make a difference. If we want to influence effectively, we need to see each of these as marginal gains we can use to bring about real long-term change. Remember, we are trying to make the best behaviour the easiest behaviour, so anything we can do to remove obstacles is beneficial. So, if choosing the right font is a marginal gain, rather than sticking with what you know, try something different.

Another marginal gain is 'micro-copy'. These are the snippets of text that guide us through a process, instruct us on how to fill in a form, and what to do next to keep us moving along. Seemingly inconsequential, micro-copy has a greater impact than you may think. Even the introduction of the single word 'because' can trigger a powerful compliance reaction. If there's an area of friction in an infosec process where things are done that shouldn't be done, it may be worth reviewing the micro-copy first.

Colour too strongly influences behaviour. In fact, how we feel about a product can be 90% down to colour alone[59]. Yellow, for instance, activates the brain's anxiety centre, while blue builds trust. And if you want to know what to avoid, what about using the world's ugliest colour[60] - a murky brown-green shade[61] - developed to put people off buying cigarettes, to nudge people away from danger?

There are lessons to be learned for infosec on how colour psychology can be used to turn someone 'on' or 'off'. Gregory Ciotti gives a detailed account of its importance and demonstrates how it can support the tone of voice you're trying to create[62]. It may be time to think a little more deeply about which you use rather than defaulting to our usual palette.

And if you think that something like colour is a mere decorative detail, just consider that Google added $200 million to its advertising revenues by merely changing the shade of blue of its toolbar[63], testing 41 variants in the process.

All this means that we cannot simply try and guess what might work in an infosec awareness campaign. We have to test, change and test again. As Stephen Dubner and Steven Levitt, authors of 'Freakonomics', put it, the hardest three words in the English language aren't "I'm sorry", or "I love you", but "I don't know"[64].

All these different communication elements need to be brought together through good design that helps make pursuing the right behaviour easier. The brain craves familiarity in unknown circumstances. Use conventions that the audience understands. Don't be creative for the sake of it. The more you make people think the less likely they are to comply. Be consistent and predictable.

Images are very much part of this. Any communication must have 'visual appeal' and look as simple and uncluttered as possible.

While words are abstract and more difficult for the brain to retain, we remember visuals much more easily and our brains process them 60,000 times faster than text[65]. Not surprisingly then that some two-thirds of us would rather learn from images and videos than text. Even tiny emojis can help make your message more memorable[66].

So, if you need to look at how you can introduce visual elements like pictures, infographics and videos into your information security awareness programmes, look at the design principles of Gestalt psychology and how you can associate images with emotions that trigger specific behaviours[67].

This chapter has been largely about small things

because small things matter. While under pressure to deliver, it's tempting to force the pace through blunt and uncompromising actions. But infosec is an ecosystem that must be nurtured through tweaks, small adjustments and adaptations that take into the account the all-too-often ignored human factor.

So, if we are to improve the 'conversion rate' when it comes to moving from old to new infosec behaviours, we must be sensitive to the day-to-day reality that employees experience in their workplace. That's something which is very much at the core of our own SABC™ programmes.

Chapter Nine

Information security is an invisible industry until something goes wrong."

Dan Ariely, behavioural economist, best-selling author

What's the Point of Infosec?

I t's obvious that information security leaders face an ever-more complex threat landscape and that this situation is likely to worsen. Not only are direct cyber attacks on the rise, but technological developments, such as the internet of things (IoT), are certain to create more challenges for which many organisations aren't prepared[68]. Increasing top-down governance and regulation in the US, Europe[69] and the UK[70] is also going to add to the pressure on CEOs and CISOs. And as there are no geographic boundaries when it comes to information security, all these issues will be playing out in their own way across South America, Africa, the Middle East, Asia and elsewhere.

With cyber crime now a $445 billion business, there are no signs that the 'bad guys' are slowing down. In fact, they are becoming more organised and aggressive.

Crises will trigger change and action. There will be further unexpected events and unexpected consequences from them. The dynamic nature of the workforce, with remote working, outsourcing and third-party contractors is adding even more complexity.

Behavioural economist Dan Ariely once described information security to me as "an invisible industry until something goes wrong."[42]

He has a point. For most of the time we are on the back foot and that makes us vulnerable. But we can't keep doing what we've always done and expect a different result. If we only ever see infosec through the prism of a people problem, our solutions will tend only to embody that blinkered perspective. If the only tool we use is a hammer, and that doesn't work, then building an even bigger one, isn't the answer.

So as security professionals, we need to meet the challenge by looking through a wider lens.

When it comes to infosec, doing nothing is no longer a neutral option. Claiming that by following standard sector practice you are only doing what everyone else does, will be no protection. To paraphrase the short and brutal riposte of one judge to such a defence: "They aren't in court. *You* are."

> *We tend to look at infosec in a reductionist way, seeing it as a set of disconnected parts, when we should see it as a system comprising culture, communications, cognitive biases, heuristics, technology and much more*

So, if we are to be more successful at changing the information security environment, we need to move away from what I see as the persistent over-concentration on technology-first solutions. This has led us to forget that people are the vital factor in the information security equation. After all, who makes, implements and maintains technology? People. And I believe it's people who provide our best opportunity for improvement. The question for our industry is how do we get the best out of them?

We can't keep presuming that people have to do what we want simply because they are employees. That means trying to impose a control-centric approach to information security seems increasingly out of step in a world where there's a continually evolving risk environment.

"The infosec community punishes imperfect solutions in an imperfect world."

Alex Stamos, CSO, Facebook

We don't want people to *think* about information security, we just want them to *do* it, so that it becomes 'just the way we do business here.' Continuing to choose the overly complex, intrusive and blunt one-size-fits-all tools we've used in the past will not effectively address this dynamic new reality.

So, if we are to take infosec initiatives to another level and achieve more satisfactory results, we need to think more deeply and differently about our policies, processes and procedures. This requires us to go beyond 'box ticking' approaches and to develop bespoke solutions that recognise the disparate behaviours of both groups and individuals within an organisation.

It also demands a change in mindset, not just among

those responsible for delivering information security, but everyone, so infosec becomes an issue that is owned by us all.

If leadership is about inspiring action, then as author Simon Sinek has said, it's also about guarding against *mis*action[71], something that's equally important in a world of volatility, uncertainty, complexity and ambiguity (VUCA).

I'm sure that some, particularly those with a vested interest in a technology-first approach, will dismiss this people-first approach as gimmicky or perhaps not relevant or feasible in a true corporate environment. But what I have tried to set out here is an approach that is underpinned by science, most particularly well-founded behavioural research that reveals how infosec habits could be significantly changed by a 'nudge in the right direction'. By using this knowledge, and new insights built up over the last 50 years, it's possible to create a better set of techniques and skills that enable others to make better choices.

As a working example of the benefits, we need look no further than the Behavioural Insights team set up by the UK government in 2010. This had the sole purpose of finding intelligent new ways to enable people to make better choices for themselves, simply because standard bureaucratic approaches were not working. Often working counter-intuitively, I think that their work can generally be regarded as a success, despite the initial scepticism of some. It was described by one journalist as "the wackiest and most vogueish corner of government"[72].

So now that decades of research by biologists,

anthropologists and psychologists has shown us how our minds work, why not use this wealth of insight to create more effective information security practices?

Behavioural research can help people to make better choices for themselves

Unfortunately, our ability to ignore the lessons of history is considerable. As renowned investor Sir John Templeton once observed, "It is different this time" are the five most expensive words in stock market history.

Some will only point out that a lot of this is common sense and disregard it as nothing special. But as we all know, common sense is often in short supply and only effective when applied. Most of the time it is not and accordingly ignored.

Hindsight bias, another of our curious cognitive quirks, also skews our judgement, causing us to disregard facts and avoid any proper analysis of root causes. And because we "knew this all along", little attempt is made to fix the situation.

But many (most) infosec campaigns are still missing a trick by not paying sufficient attention to the vagaries of human nature. With that said, I do see a slight turning of the tide and a growing acceptance in our industry that awareness, behaviour and culture can have a greater role to play in creating more information-secure organisations. Some organisations are choosing to build the competencies they need in-house, while others are reaching out to organisations like Marmalade Box to source the skills and support they need.

Awareness, behaviour and culture are certainly at the core of our own SABC™ methodology, which has been built very much on identifying and analysing the root causes of non-compliance.

And my own experience working with companies and organisations across a range of sectors both in the UK and Europe has proven to me, and to them, that incorporating science, best practice and psychological insights, some of which I've touched upon here, can help inform policy and process design.

We have shown that when approached with creativity and insight, even stubborn risks can be engineered out of the system. So, we have used the SABC™ structured approach in organisations around the world to help their staff acquire not just better awareness of security risks, but to do so in ways that bring about significant changes in infosec behaviour *without* resorting to throwing ever more technology at the problem.

Since behaviour alters slowly, you need to give people the best chance to change. That's why we work with most of our clients on three-year-long infosec programmes that move them closer to becoming information secure. This gives sufficient opportunity for people to adopt new behaviours. As I've mentioned before, there is no quick fix to embedding better information security behaviours. So, having the time to test, tweak and refine infosec programmes to suit the needs of the organisation is imperative, if we are to obtain the results we desire.

The first year, while tailored to the organisation, is more generic than specific. It removes the 'big rocks' from the system and lays the foundations for what is to come. By the second year, we have been able to identify the areas of greatest resistance and non-change, the vital information we need to create the following year's programme of specific targeted intervention. This 'nudge' approach gives many the best opportunity to change.

By the end of the third year, we can see how this programme has worked. Most problems will have been resolved, but some won't, and these will require another round of intervention, based on the behavioural and cultural insights we've gained. This continues until we reach a point where there are no longer any areas of non-compliance. Or, despite the extra love they've received, those who are 'infosec resistant' have self-identified through their unresponsiveness.

There will always be those in life who are innately non-compliant. Those who speed. Those who fail to wear seatbelts. Those who never exercise. Those who fail to plan for their retirement. They all demonstrate the human in-built resistance to being changed against their will.

It merely highlights the difficulty of getting everyone 'on side'. And just as with driving, periodically testing someone's abilities will not reveal their bad driving habits when they are out on their own.

So, we should not be surprised if, when it comes to information security, our attempts to retrain don't always go well. In fact, we need to accept that there will always be mavericks who cannot, whatever is done, make the transition from 'infosec denier' to 'security convert'. Just as with the driving test, despite being given the same training, some pass and others fail.

And what do you do when you encounter someone who won't or can't comply? It's a business decision as to whether they remain or have no place in the organisation, even if they are your best salespeople. So that it catches no one by surprise, I would always advise putting in place, at the very start of any infosec programme, a governance process to define how you will progress when you hit a barrier — and at some point, you *will* hit a barrier.

Behavioural economics and choice architecture aren't just esoteric disciplines but powerful tools we can use to influence how others behave when presented with different options

Is it possible to distil the contents of this book into an action plan?

Every situation is different, so the complexity of challenges that individual organisations present make it impossible to prescribe a 'human factor action plan' in any meaningful detail. But I think it is possible to identify some guiding principles that a CISO, or anyone else responsible for information security, can use to bring about behavioural change.

The most obvious is to seriously give the human factor greater priority from now on. It will be tempting, particularly when under pressure, to opt for the security blanket of technology as the go-to response. But do that, and it will be difficult to get beyond first base. So, start thinking now about what you have read in this book and how it could be applied to your organisation. For instance, think about where the 'behavioural bear traps' lie and how you might use some of the insights to avoid them.

Making any transition from the status quo is always difficult. Try to move too fast and you will be met by resistance, some foreseen, but probably much that is not. As we've seen, people don't like change, even when it's for the better. So, we shouldn't always try to get to where we want to be in one go. That may not please those demanding immediate change, but it does reflect behavioural reality. That's why providing solutions to smaller problems can be a good start point, building trust and gaining acceptance, as people's behaviour is repositioned using a series of stepping stones.

The success of the British cycling team shows how we shouldn't be frightened to think small. It's tempting to believe that only big breakthroughs make a difference and that pursuing them is the only game in town. But if we get swept away on a wave of enthusiasm for lofty distant goals, we forget about the small actions that shape and reinforce people's behaviour on a daily basis. Yet it's in these areas of marginal gain that often we need to look if we want to move forward.

Certainly, when it comes to making 'the best behaviour the easiest behaviour', small steps are often key. So, if we can design new infosec campaigns that dampen the moments of pain and unpleasantness while maximising the moments of pleasure, we will be well on our way to nudging people in the right direction.

There will always be tasks that people don't want to do at the best of times. Complying with information security best practice is probably one of them. We should accept this, but not seek to make our lives any harder. But that's exactly what we do when we follow the well-trodden path of thinking we can change the quality of behaviour through the quantity of information we provide. Linguist Steven Pinker calls this tendency among technical people to 'dump' too much information too soon 'the curse of knowledge', and it just doesn't work.

It's been said that if you create a great experience, people remember it and want to experience it again. On the other hand, build a bad one and people never want to experience it again. I fear that all too often we do the latter.

Instead, we need to see ourselves as being in an information security marketplace that requires us to create a product that people will buy. When infosec campaigns fail, it's our fault, not that of our audience. Where possible, this requires us to create tailored content and material that speaks in the right way to those who consume it. To do that, we must appreciate that often it's emotion and illogic, rather than rationality and argument, that unlocks behavioural change.

So, if a person's behaviour doesn't seem to make sense, it's probably because we aren't seeing the 'invisible' barriers that stop them from acting in the way we want. The specific situation someone finds themselves in may have a greater impact on behaviour than we think and determine what we do more than our personality or intelligence[73]. Having a greater understanding of these underlying mechanisms, such as cognitive bias, enables us to be better choice architects[74] when it comes to creating the context in which people make decisions about information security awareness.

If we look to the marketplace again, we can see that those who are most successful connect to their customers through common ground. They are tuned into the needs of their buyers, who accordingly can see 'what's in it for them'. While we don't have a sexy consumer good to offer them, we should at least be selling to our audience a sense of shared endeavour. That as individuals and collectively we are looking to do the right thing. Often that sense isn't there because of a lack of understanding about what infosec is and why it matters to everyone.

McGill University cites its STARS programme (Science Talks About Research for Staff), in which professors described their work to secretaries, bookkeepers and administrators far removed from actual science, as injecting a much greater sense of pride among those in the organisation.

Of course, none of this is to say that we should put all our proverbial eggs in the behavioural basket. We still lack an accurate map of the human mind, which makes predicting our behaviour notoriously difficult, as pollsters on both sides of the pond discovered in 2016. But we are swiftly developing a better understanding of how to press the right buttons to bring about the most effective and sustainable changes in behaviour.

At industry-wide level, perhaps we need to agree a standard for what we mean by awareness, behaviour and culture that will enable us to benchmark our own bespoke metrics against this. With universally accepted parameters in place, we would then create a competitive arena that would help drive performance standards upwards, just as in sport, where champions swap world records.

How easy would it be to define such standards? We won't know until we try. But if awareness, behaviour and culture are important in information security, they should be on our risk register and not ignored because they are seen as too abstract to measure and manage.

And after all, abstract concepts like time and distance have been calculated for millennia.

Of course, we can never expect to be 100% secure. We can only ever shift the risk balance more in our favour. There will always be problems, there will always be threats and this puts us in a war we can in effect never win.

This means that information security initiatives are always a work in progress that need continual tweaking and adjustment to counter risks both outside the organisation and within it.

When I began writing this book, the Facebook privacy scandal was very much in the news. An event very much of its own making. But despite such dark clouds, Facebook appeared at one-time Teflon-coated with its share price rising from a low of $152.22 during the depth of the recent crisis, to hit an all-time high just three months later. However, this summer respite was short-lived when on Wednesday, July 25th 2018, Facebook saw $119bn wiped off it's value, the worst one-day fall in stock market history.

Inevitably, other information breaches will erupt on the scene. They always do, and, it's these big picture events that tend to capture the headlines and clearly demonstrate how corporate attitudes to risk are reflected in major decisions taken at the top.

But every day around the world, millions of workers make information security choices, which though much smaller, nevertheless put their organisation in harm's way, leaving it vulnerable and exposed to data breaches and cyber attack. They don't do this through any intent or ill will, but simply because they are human and so are open to a range of common, powerful influences that affect their behaviour. If we understand and appreciate what these are we will be much better equipped to prevent them from making potentially faulty judgements.

People may be the problem, but they are also the answer.

References

Chapter 1 - The Case For Change

1 Advanced Persistent Threat Activity Targeting Energy and Other Critical Infrastructure Sectors, 2018.
www.us-cert.gov/ncas/alerts/TA17-293A

2 House of Commons Culture, Media and Sport Committee Cyber Security: Protection of Personal Data Online First Report of Session 2016–17
https://publications.parliament.uk/pa/cm201617/cms-elect/cmcumeds/148/148.pdf

3 Zuckerberg takes Facebook data apology tour to Washington
www.cnet.com/news/mark-zuckerberg-takes-facebook-data-apology-tour-to-washington-congress-cambridge-analytica/

4 Cyber-attack Volume Doubled in First Half of 2017
www.infosecurity-magazine.com/news/cyberattack-
volume-doubled-2017/

Chapter 2 - A Scan of the Information Security Landscape

5 Cyber security breaches survey April 2017
https://assets.publishing.service.gov.uk/government/upl
oads/system/uploads/attachment_data/file/609186/Cy
ber_Security_Breaches_Survey_2017_main_report_PU
BLIC.pdf

6 86% of Customers Would Shun Brands Following a
Data Breach
https://semafone.com/press-releases/86-customers-
shun-brands-following-data-breach/

7 Ponemon Institute's 2017 Cost of Data Breach Study:
Global Overview
www-01.ibm.com/common/ssi/cgi-bin/ssialias?html-
fid=SEL03130WWEN

8 The Reputational Impact of IT Risk
www-
935.ibm.com/services/multimedia/RLL12363USEN.pdf

9 The Aftermath of a Mega Data Breach: Consumer
Sentiment
www.experian.com/assets/p/data-breach/experian-
consumer-study-on-aftermath-of-a-data-breach.pdf

10 SWIFT - Global banking under attack
www.scmagazineuk.com/2-minutes-on-swift--global-
banking-under-attack/article/532276/

11 Silicon Valley Has Failed to Protect Our Data. Here's
How to Fix It
www.bloomberg.com/news/articles/2018-03-21/paul-
ford-facebook-is-why-we-need-a-digital-protection-
agency

12 Senator John Kennedy Quoted on Twitter
https://twitter.com/SenJohnKennedy/status/97610562
9935919104

13 ENISA. Threat and Risk Management
www.enisa.europa.eu/topics/threat-risk-management

14 Information Security Analysts
www.bls.gov/ooh/computer-and-information-
technology/information-security-analysts.htm

15 Information Security Budgets: More Money and
More Staff, But Growth Finally Slowing
www.cebglobal.com/blogs/information-security-
budgets-more-money-and-more-staff-but-growth-finally-
slowing/

16 2017 Global Information Security Workforce Study
Benchmarking Workforce Capacity and Response to
Cyber Risk
https://iamcybersafe.org/wp-
content/uploads/2017/06/Europe-GISWS-Report.pdf

17 Number Of Americans Quitting Their Jobs Surges To Highest In 16 Years
www.zerohedge.com/news/2017-03-16/americans-quitting-their-jobs-surges-highest-16-years

Chapter 3 - Everything's a Product ... Including Security

18 Edelman Trust Barometer 2016
www.edelman.com/insights/intellectual-property/2016-edelman-trust-barometer/state-of-trust/employee-trust-divide/

19 Millennials: The Job-Hopping Generation
http://news.gallup.com/businessjournal/191459/millennials-job-hopping-generation.aspx

20 Millennials projected to overtake Baby Boomers as America's largest generation
www.pewresearch.org/fact-tank/2018/03/01/millennials-overtake-baby-boomers/

21 Neurogenesis and the spacing effect: Learning over time enhances memory and the survival of new neurons
www.ncbi.nlm.nih.gov/pmc/articles/PMC1876761/

22 Stamos preaches defensive security research in Black Hat keynote
https://searchsecurity.techtarget.com/news/450423451/Stamos-preaches-defensive-security-research-in-Black-Hat-keynote

Chapter 4 - Creating a New Awareness Culture

23 Why "Company Culture" Is a Misleading Term
https://hbr.org/2015/04/why-company-culture-is-a-misleading-term

24 How Long Does it Actually Take to Form a New Habit? (Backed by Science)
https://jamesclear.com/new-habit

25 Cyber Security Breaches Survey 2018
https://assets.publishing.service.gov.uk/government/uploads/system/uploads/attachment_data/file/702074/Cyber_Security_Breaches_Survey_2018_-_Main_Report.pdf

Chapter 5 - Creating Diversity

26 Why Diverse Teams Are Smarter
https://hbr.org/2016/11/why-diverse-teams-are-smarter

27 Labor Force Statistics from the Current Population Survey
www.bls.gov/cps/cpsaat11.htm

28 Women in Security: Wisely Positioned for the Future of InfoSec
www.isc2.org/-/media/40970831EAB44E2A851D2D-BA51EA24E1.ashx

29 Segregated Valley: the ugly truth about Google and diversity in tech
www.theguardian.com/technology/2017/aug/07/sili-con-valley-google-diversity-black-women-workers

30 Global Information Security Workforce Study 2017 Benchmarking Workforce Capacity and Response to Cyber Risk
https://iamcybersafe.org/wp-content/uploads/2017/06/Europe-GISWS-Report.pdf

31 (ISC)2 at a crossroads: CISSP value vs. security industry growth
https://searchsecurity.techtarget.com/opinion/ISC2-at-a-crossroads-CISSP-value-vs-security-industry-growth

32 Diverse Teams Feel Less Comfortable — and That's Why They Perform Better
http://hbr.org/2016/09/diverse-teams-feel-less-comfortable-and-thats-why-they-perform-better

33 The Biases That Punish Racially Diverse Teams
https://hbr.org/2016/02/the-biases-that-punish-racially-diverse-teams

34 Why Diversity Matters
www.mckinsey.com/business-functions/organiza-tion/our-insights/why-diversity-matters

35 Gender diversity within R&D teams: Its impact on radicalness of innovation
www.tandfonline.com/doi/abs/10.5172/impp.2013.15.2.149

Chapter 6 - Better Behaviour By Design

36 Email Statistics Report, 2015-2019
www.radicati.com/wp/wp-content/up-
loads/2015/02/Email-Statistics-Report-2015-2019-
Executive-Summary.pdf

37 The Modern Corporate Learner
www.mlevel.com/wp-
content/uploads/2017/01/mLevel_Modern_Corpo-
rate_Learner.pdf

38 The Checklist Manifesto - How to Get Things Right
http://atulgawande.com/book/the-checklist-manifesto/

39 You make 35,000 decisions a day, and Huawei wants
AI to help out
https://uk.news.yahoo.com/35-000-decisions-day-
huawei-204525823.html?guccounter=1

40 Basecamp Employee Handbook
https://github.com/basecamp/handbook/blob/master/
README.md

Chapter 7 - Changing Behaviour Without Changing Minds

41 The Backfire Effect
https://youarenotsosmart.com/2011/06/10/the-
backfire-effect/

Chapter 8 - Managing the Message

42 Behavioural Change in Cybersecurity, with Dan Ariely
www.marmaladebox.com/podcast/behavioural-change-dan-ariely/

43 Stanford's School Of Persuasion: BJ Fogg On How To Win Users And Influence Behavior
www.forbes.com/sites/anthonykos-ner/2012/12/04/stanfords-school-of-persuasion-bj-fogg-on-how-to-win-users-and-influence-behavior/#1da159dd390d

44 Provision of social norm feedback to high prescribers of antibiotics in general practice: a pragmatic national randomised controlled trial
www.ncbi.nlm.nih.gov/pmc/articles/PMC4842844/

45 Neural correlates of maintaining one's political beliefs in the face of counterevidence
www.nature.com/articles/srep39589

46 How Uber Uses Psychological Tricks to Push Its Drivers' Buttons
www.nytimes.com/interactive/2017/04/02/technolo-gy/uber-drivers-psychological-tricks.html?emc=edit_n-n_20170403&nl=morning-briefi

47 How we form habits, change existing ones
www.sciencedaily.com/releas-es/2014/08/140808111931.htm

48 How To Change Someone's Mind, According To Science
www.fastcompany.com/3058314/how-to-change-some-ones-mind-according-to-science

49 Everyday Empathy
https://medium.com/mule-design/everyday-empathy-6a475e03fd81

50 How to connect with your audience, with Ben Afia
www.marmaladebox.com/podcast/connect-with-your-audience/

51 New Survey Identifies the Hottest Trends in Corp Comm and PR; Announcing the 2018 JOTW Communications Survey
www.swordandthescript.com/2018/03/jotw-pr-corporate-communications-survey/

52 Your Brain on Fiction
www.nytimes.com/2012/03/18/opinion/sunday/the-neuroscience-of-your-brain-on-fiction.html

53 The Definitive Guide to Reading Microexpressions
www.scienceofpeople.com/microexpressions/

54 Optimizely: Split Testing Simplified http://www.optimizely.com/optimization-glossary/split-testing/?redir=uk

55 The Aesthetics of Reading
https://affect.media.mit.edu/pdfs/05.larson-picard.pdf

56 If It's Hard to Read, It's Hard to Do. Processing Fluency Affects Effort Prediction and Motivation https://dornsife.usc.edu/assets/sites/780/docs/08_ps_s ong___schwarz_effort.pdf

57 An Eye Tracking Study of How Font Size and Type Influence Online Reading www.bcs.org/upload/pdf/ewic_hc08_v2_paper4.pdf

58 Font Size Matters—Emotion and Attention in Cortical Responses to Written Words http://journals.plos.org/plosone/article? id=10.1371/journal.pone.0036042

59 Impact of color on marketing www.emeraldinsight.- com/doi/abs/10.1108/00251740610673332%20

60 'World's ugliest colour' used on cigarette packets to put smokers off www.independent.co.uk/news/world/australa- sia/worlds-ugliest-colour-revealed-pantone-448c- a7076446.html

61 The Ugliest Colour www.pantone.com/color-finder/448-C

62 The Psychology of Color in Marketing and Branding www.entrepreneur.com/article/233843

63 Why Google has 200m reasons to put engineers over designers
www.theguardian.com/technology/2014/feb/05/why-google-engineers-designers

64 The Three Hardest Words in the English Language: Full Transcript
http://freakonomics.com/2014/05/15/the-three-hardest-words-in-the-english-language-full-transcript/

65 Humans Process Visual Data Better
http://www.t-sciences.com/news/humans-process-visual-data-better

66 These Emojis Can Increase Click-Through Rates, According to New Data
https://blog.hubspot.com/marketing/best-emojis

67 Simplicity, symmetry and more: Gestalt theory and the design principles it gave birth to
https://www.canva.com/learn/gestalt-theory/

Chapter 9 - What's the Point of Infosec?

68 How much is the Internet of everything worth? Cisco says $19 trillion
www.cnet.com/news/how-much-is-the-internet-of-everything-worth-cisco-says-19-trillion/

69 General Data Protection Regulation (GDPR)
www.eugdpr.org/

70 Matt Hancock's speech on technology at the Margaret Thatcher Conference on Security
www.gov.uk/government/speeches/matt-hancocks-speech-on-technology-at-the-margaret-thatcher-conference-on-security

71 Why good leaders make you feel safe, Simon Sinek
www.ted.com/talks/simon_sinek_why_good_leaders_-make_you_feel_safe

72 Effective things can come from silly places
www.theguardian.com/commentis-free/2011/jul/08/bad-science-effective-things-silly-places

73 Predicting more of the people more of the time: Assessing the personality of situations.
http://psycnet.apa.org/record/1979-28632-001

74 Thaler Explains How "Choice Architecture" Makes the World a Better Place
www.chicagobooth.edu/news/2008mancon/01-thaler.aspx

Using the SABC™ Framework

If you're interested in adopting the SABC™ Framework in your organisation you have the following options;

1. Partner with Marmalade Box
Work with Marmalade Box so that they can guide and support you as you implement it in your organisation. Find out more at www.marmaladebox.com

2. Train Your Team
You can put your team through our SABC™ training so that they can implement it in your organisation.

Find out more about our SABC™ training at www.marmaladebox.com/SABC-training

3. Hire a SABC Approved Associate
We train independent security professionals in SABC™.

Get in touch through Marmalade Box with your requirements.

About the Author

Bruce Hallas is an information and cyber security expert who loves to ponder the challenges of our time and get under the skin of why we do what we do. His forward thinking ideas are why he's invited to speak around the world on cybersecurity and human behaviour.

He is the Founder and Chief Strategist at Marmalade Box, an info sec consultancy that helps design security processes that reduce the guesswork from the human factor. Marmalade Box partner with businesses around the world to help them embed a security culture within their organisations.

Bruce is also the founder of The Analogies Project, an online collection of infosec analogies written by voluntary contribution.

Bruce dreams of living by the sea with his family so that he can continue to ponder and get some sailing in!

 twitter.com/brucehallas

Work with Bruce

Consulting

If you would like Bruce to consult on your project, you can reach him at consulting@brucehallas.com

Speaking

If you would like Bruce to speak at your event or conference please send an email to speaker@brucehallas.com

Coaching & Mentoring

Bruce takes on a limited number of coaching and mentoring clients. If you would like to apply then please send an email to coaching@brucehallas.com

The Analogies Project

The Analogies Project is an online library of analogies for security professionals to use in communicating the information security story.

This open source collection - written by voluntary contribution - uses storytelling, analogies and metaphors to draw parallels between information security, and historical and everyday occurrences.

You can find out more about The Analogies Project at theanalogiesproject.org

Additional Resources

Re-thinking the Human Factor Podcast

Listen to Bruce's podcast about information security awareness, behaviour and culture for information security professionals.

Bruce interviews guests from outside the security industry who specialise in aspects of awareness, behaviour and culture and invites them to share how they have effectively tackled the challenges we face as security professionals.

Listen on Spotify, Apple Podcasts or via the Marmalade Box website at www.marmaladebox.com

Also by Bruce Hallas

Bruce is also a co-author of

Cyber Security ABCs: Delivering Awareness, Behaviours and Culture change

Cyber security issues, problems and incidents don't always relate to technological faults. Many can be avoided or mitigated through improved cyber security awareness, behaviour and culture change (ABCs). This book guides organisations looking to create an enhanced security culture through improved understanding and practice of cyber security at an individual level. Crucial concepts are covered from the ground up, alongside tools to measure key indicators and enable organisational change.

Publisher: BCS, The Chartered Institute for IT

ISBN-10: 1780174241

ISBN-13: 978-1780174242